ME AND MY CAMERA

JOE PARTRIDGE

ASH & GRANT

Me and My Camera was produced, edited, and designed
by Dorling Kindersley Limited, 9 Henrietta Street,
London WC2.

Editor **Richard Dawes**
Art Director **Stuart Jackman**
Design Assistant **Rosamund Gendle**

Ash & Grant,
9 Henrietta Street, London WC2

'Ash & Grant' is a registered imprint of
Dorling Kindersley Ltd
First Published 1981. Fourth impression 1981.
Revised edition published 1983.

British Library Cataloguing in Publication Data
Partridge, Joe
Me and My Camera. – Rev. ed.
1. Photography
I. Title
770'.28   TR 146
ISBN   0-904069-49-4

For Peter, Sue, and Carole and everyone else on the top of the
Clapham omnibus who owns a camera.

ME AND MY CAMERA

Joe Partridge is the main presenter of the Yorkshire Television series *Me and My Camera*. A keen amateur photographer for years, he left the business world for a full-time career in photography, and graduated from Bournemouth and Poole College of Art's School of Photography. Joe now works mainly for newspapers, including the *Sunday Times*, magazines, and books.

He broadcasts on photography on LBC Radio's *London Life* magazine programme, covering the whole range of subjects of interest to the amateur camera user, and on BBC Radio 1's *Staying Alive*. Joe also contributes a regular column to a top-selling photographic magazine, as well as features for a range of popular publications.

CONTENTS

FOREWORD TO THE REVISED EDITION

I had been reviewing photography books for LBC Radio for several years before the chance came to present *Me and My Camera* for Yorkshire Television and to write this book. Every month a heap of "How-to-do-it" books landed on my desk, each packed full of technical data and exotic equipment. But there was nothing for the person who wanted to take better snapshots of their holidays, family, and friends.

Me and My Camera gave me the opportunity to address just that sort of person. My original title for the book was "Family Photography" and since it was published I have met hundreds of families where everyone had got some help from it.

Your camera should be used to record the things you do, but not control them. By learning the basic techniques you will soon be taking better pictures and be able to get on with the business of living.

This revised edition has allowed me to talk about some of the latest cameras, including the new instant picture models and the exciting Disc cameras. But don't let all the buttons and dials on modern cameras put you off. It's all getting simpler, really, and with care you will take wonderful photographs.

One shot out of a series of 25-second exposures, caught just the effect Joe Partridge was looking for. Shooting outdoors is the best way to do justice to lighting like this, but be careful in electrical storms.

INTRODUCTION

This book is for everyone who owns a camera, or would like to use one. Like the Yorkshire Television programme on which it is based, its aim is to help you understand better what your camera can do, and learn to make use of the techniques of experienced photographers in your own pictures. It is also designed to serve as a ready source of advice, information, and picture-taking tips when you are out with your camera.

A very famous photographer once told me that the three most important rules of good photography were: "Get closer – Get closer – Get closer." His advice illustrates the first principle in photography:

Heather Angel used a lightweight survival blanket to throw additional light on the woodland fungi in the picture, left. She preferred the gentle light it gave to harsh direct flash light.

Fireworks have great potential for spectacular night time shots, but exposure is critical here if colour is to be faithful. George Hughes took the picture, above.

it is not your camera that takes good pictures, it is *you*. Whether you own a pocket model or an advanced single lens reflex, it is still only a light-tight box with a hole in one end and a piece of sensitive film in the other. Don't be nervous of your equipment, or of the technicalities of photography. The way you see the world is far more important.

The book has four main sections. The first explains how different cameras operate, and the choice of films, flash equipment, filters and accessories to suit your needs. The second shows you how to handle your camera controls, and use them creatively, and with confidence. The fourth section contains extra information on many aspects of photography, from filter types to presenting your pictures. All these sections concentrate on basic, practical information.

The third, and largest section gives you advice on photographing different subjects. As in the TV programme, each major theme is introduced by a look at the approach of a well-known photographer – Patrick Lichfield on people and portraits, George Hughes at a wedding, Derry Brabbs on landscape, Chris Smith on sport, Heather Angel on nature, and Homer Sykes on the urban environment, with myself on approaches to holiday and travel shots. By looking at their photographs, which are also featured here, and at the many other pictures in this book, you will gain inspiration for your own photography.

The sense of distance in Derry Brabbs' study of a disused South Wales coal mine, below, conveys the forlorn quality of a once-powerful force.

The group portrait of the
Royal Family was taken
by Patrick Lichfield.

Chris Smith's picture,
left, gives the feel of
action even though the
subject is stationary.
The lack of distraction in
the background makes
the subject more
dynamic.

GLOSSARY

Accessory shoe Metal or plastic fitting, usually on top of a camera, for holding flash guns or other accessories. It does not connect the flash gun to the camera shutter. See Hot shoe.

Angle of view The widest angle through which a lens can accept light and still give a full *format* image on the film.

Aperture The opening in the lens, fixed on simple cameras but adjustable on others, that controls the amount of light reaching the film.

Aperture priority camera Automatic 35 mm camera on which the user selects the aperture and the camera sets the appropriate shutter speed.

Artificial light Light other than daylight. Usually provided by flash, but sometimes by *tungsten light* bulbs.

ASA (American Standards Association) Measurement of a film's sensitivity to light. The higher the ASA the faster, or more sensitive, the film.

Autofocus camera Camera that uses a sound or light pulse to measure the distance between camera and subject, and then automatically focuses the lens before taking the picture.

Automatic camera Camera which automatically sets the aperture and/or shutter speed for a correct *exposure*.

Automatic electronic flash Flash gun with a sensor that measures the light bouncing back from the subject, so that the gun can cut off the flash when enough has been delivered.

Available light Any light other than that added by the photographer.

"B" (Bulb) Shutter speed setting which keeps the shutter open as long as the button is depressed. Used for exposures longer than the numbered settings. Has largely replaced the "T" (Time) setting.

Back light Light coming towards the camera lens from behind the subject.

Bounced flash A method of getting a softer, more diffused light from a flash gun by bouncing the light off a white wall or ceiling on to the subject.

Bracketing Method of ensuring correct exposure by taking several pictures of the same subject with a range of settings.

Cable release A flexible extension to the shutter release of a camera that allows you to fire the shutter without the risk of jogging the camera.

Cartridge Preloaded plastic film container used in 110 or 126 cameras. It slots straight into the camera, and can be removed without rewinding.

Cassette Light-tight film container made of metal or plastic and used with 35 mm cameras. After the film is finished, it is rewound into the cassette.

Centre-weighted meter A form of camera light meter that reads light from the whole subject, but gives more emphasis to the central area.

Colour negative film Film which gives only colour prints.

Colour transparency film Film which gives colour slides for projection or viewing. Prints can be made from these slides, but the process is expensive. Also known as *Reversal film*.

Compact camera Small, fixed-lens 35 mm camera with a viewfinder separate from the lens.

Composition The arrangement of the elements of a photograph.

Coupled rangefinder *Rangefinder* linked to the camera's focusing control.

DIN The German equivalent of *ASA*.

Daylight film Film designed for use in daylight, or with electronic flash or blue flash bulbs.

Depth of field The amount of a picture that will appear sharp in front of and behind the point on which you focus.

Depth of field preview Button on a camera that closes the lens down to the *working aperture*, so that you can see how much of the picture will be in focus.

Depth of field scale Set of marks on a lens to enable the photographer to calculate the *depth of field* for any aperture.

Disc camera A camera of flat design that uses circular film, normally with fifteen exposures.

Distance symbols Symbols used to indicate focusing positions.

Electronic flash Flash gun that produces light by passing an electric charge along a tube. Provides a reusable source of light.

Emulsion The light-sensitive material that is coated on different bases to make photographic film or paper.

Enlargement Any print larger than the negative used to produce it. The term is more commonly used to denote a print bigger than an *en-print*.

En-print Standard size print made on $3\frac{1}{2}$ ins wide paper from any popular negative size.

Exposure The combination of the time for which light is allowed to fall on a film and the intensity of that light. The time is determined by the *shutter speed*, the intensity by the *aperture* setting.

Exposure compensator Device which overrides the controls of an *automatic camera*, allowing deliberate *underexposure* or *overexposure*.

Exposure setting The setting of a camera's aperture and shutter speed controls for a correct exposure.

f stop Indication of the size of apertures on a camera lens. The higher the number, the smaller the size of aperture.

Fast film Film with a high sensitivity to light and a high ASA number. It is suitable for poor light conditions, but produces grainy results.

Fast lens Lens with a wide maximum aperture.

Fill-in Flash or reflector used to lighten the shadows in a picture.

Film Photographic material consisting of a light-sensitive *emulsion* coated on a plastic base.

Film frame counter Numbered display on a camera body showing how many pictures have been taken on the film.

Film speed The sensitivity of a film to light. Films are given ASA numbers which denote their speed. The higher the ASA, the more sensitive the film.

Filter Lens attachment made of transparent material such as glass or plastic, which alters the nature, colour, or quality of the light passing through it.

Fixed focus Term describing a camera that has no method of focusing the lens. Many cheap cameras use this system, which allows subjects at distances over 6 ft to appear reasonably sharp on the film.

Fixed lens Lens permanently attached to a camera.

Flare Unwanted light scattered by reflections within the lens or camera interior. It can reduce image contrast and shadow detail.

Flash cube Cube containing four flash bulbs. When the film is wound on, the cube rotates to bring another bulb into the firing position.

Flash guide number Number which provides a guide to the correct exposure when using flash.

Flash sensor Device which measures the amount of flash light reflected from the subject, allowing the flash gun to control the light's intensity and duration.

Flash synchronization Method of ensuring that flash light duration and the maximum camera shutter opening coincide. Many cameras have two synchronization settings: M for bulb flash and X for electronic flash.

Flipflash Flash unit containing several bulbs, allowing you to fire up to four at once, to increase flash strength.

Focal length The effective distance from lens to film, measured in millimeters. The primary classification of lenses is by their focal length. Long focal length gives a narrow *angle of view*, reduced *depth of field*, and increased subject size. Short focal length gives a wide angle of view, increased depth of field, and reduced subject size.

Focus The point at which light rays passing through a lens converge to give a clear, sharp image of the subject.

Focusing screen Ground glass or plastic screen in a camera which allows the image to be viewed and focused.

Format Size of film negative, photographic paper, or viewing area.

Grain Metallic silver particles in film which form a visible photographic image when the film is exposed and developed.

Granularity The amount of *grain* clumping that occurrs within a film *emulsion* during development, forming the final image.

Highlights The brightest, lightest areas in a subject or photograph.

Hot shoe Fitting on a camera which provides a fastening for a flash gun, and links the gun to the camera's shutter.

Infinity The focusing position at which distant objects are in focus.

Instant picture camera Camera which produces a processed photograph within minutes of the film being exposed.

LCD (or Liquid crystal diode) Indicator used in a camera viewfinder to convey information about *exposure*, flash readiness, etc.

LED (Light-emitting diode) Viewfinder indicator light, similar in function to an LCD.

Lens Optical device made of glass or plastic capable of bending light. Camera lenses gather light rays reflected from the subject to form an image on the film.

Lens hood Opaque tube, usually metal or rubber, that prevents unwanted light falling on the lens surface.

Light meter Accessory for measuring light intensity and calculating correct exposure. Also known as an exposure meter.

Macro lens Camera lens designed especially to give high image quality in close-up photography.

Magicube *Flash cube* fired mechanically, for cameras that do not take batteries.

Motor drive Mechanism, either built-in to a camera or added as an accessory, that winds on the film and recocks the shutter after each picture.

Multimode camera 35 mm camera which offers a choice of up to six different exposure systems, or "modes" These usually include *aperture priority*, *shutter priority*, manual, and automatic.

Natural light Light originating from a natural source, such as the sun.

Negative Developed photographic image in which light areas in the subject appear dark, and shadows appear light. It is usually made on a transparent base, so that an image with normal, positive tones can be printed by exposing sensitive paper to light which passes through it.

Normal lens A lens with a *focal length* approximately equal to the diagonal measurement of the film *format* with which it is used. Also known as a standard lens.

Off-camera flash Flash gun mounted or held separately from the camera.

Overexposure The result of giving the film excessive *exposure* to light. Produces a weakening of colour, or a lightening of tones in black and white pictures.

Panchromatic Term describing photographic film or paper which is sensitive to all the colours of the visible spectrum.

Panning The technique of swinging the camera to follow a moving subject, so that the main subject will be sharp and the background blurred.

Parallax error The difference between the image area seen through a camera's *viewfinder*, and that recorded by the film. Cameras with *TTL (through-the-lens)* viewing avoid this error.

Perspective System of representing three-dimensional objects on a two-dimensional surface to give depth.

Rangefinder Built-in focusing aid in some 35 mm compact cameras. It shows a double or split image in the viewfinder until the subject is in focus.

Reflector Device for bouncing light, to give indirect illumination of the subject.

Reprint *En-print* made from the *negative* after the first set of prints has been produced.

Reversal film Film designed to produce a positive result directly from exposure and processing, without a negative.

SLR (Single lens reflex) Camera which allows the user to see the exact image

formed by the picture-taking lens, by means of a system of mirrors between lens and film.

Self timer Device on some cameras providing a timed delay between the activation and firing of the shutter. Allows the photographer to include himself in the picture.

Shutter System controlling the amount of time light can act on a film.

Shutter priority camera Automatic 35 mm camera on which the user selects the shutter speed and the camera sets the appropriate lens aperture.

Shutter speed Amount of time (usually measured in fractions of a second) for which a camera shutter remains open, allowing light to act on the film.

Skylight filter *Filter*, usually very pale pink, used in colour photography to reduce blue casts associated with skylight. It can be left on the lens permanently to protect it.

Slide Positive image produced on transparent film for projection on a screen. Also known as a transparency.

Slow film Film with a low sensitivity to light and a low *ASA* number. It is best for use in bright conditions. Minimal *grain* is evident.

Slow lens Lens with a small maximum *aperture*.

Split image Focusing aid in the viewfinder of most 35 mm SLR cameras that splits the image horizontally until the subject is in focus.

Standard lens See Normal lens.

Stopping down Setting a smaller lens aperture, to allow less light to enter the lens, but to produce greater *depth of field*.

Supplementary lens Additional lens attached to a camera's *normal lens* to provide a different focal length.

Telephoto lens Lens of long *focal length* which enlarges distant subjects within its narrow *angle of view*.

Transparency See Slide.

Tripod Three-legged camera stand used when it is important to keep the camera steady.

TTL (through-the-lens) metering Light metering system using light-sensitive cells within the camera body to measure light which has passed through the lens.

Tungsten light Artificial light source using a tungsten filament contained within a glass envelope.

Tungsten film Colour film suitable for use with *tungsten light* sources.

UV (Ultraviolet) filter *Filter* used to reduce the effects of ultraviolet radiation.

Underexposure The result of giving a film insufficient exposure to light. Produces a darkening of the image.

Viewfinder Window in a camera body allowing the photographer to view, compose, and sometimes also focus the image. It usually also displays exposure information.

Wide-angle lens Lens of a short focal length, which gives a wide angle of view.

Working aperture The preselected *aperture* setting which comes into operation only when the shutter is released. This allows framing and focusing at maximum aperture, for optimum brightness, with SLR cameras.

X flash synchronization Camera setting which ensures that the maximum shutter opening coincides with the firing of an electronic flash gun.

Zoom lens Lens constructed to allow continuously variable focal length within a certain range.

UNDERSTANDING CAMERAS, FILMS AND ACCESSORIES

110 CAMERAS

Most 110 cameras are inexpensive, lightweight, and fit your pocket or bag. All take an easy-loading film cartridge and the most basic are simple to use, with just a sensitive shutter release and a connection for cube or bar flash. More sophisticated models have their own electronic flash and built-in motor wind and rewind. They may also have built-in supplementary lenses that allow you to take close-ups or to fill the frame with the subject, and focusing aids. Most of these models have exposure controls for dull and sunny weather, and on some exposure is automatic. The top-priced 110s offer a choice of lenses and accessories.

Weather symbols

Shutter release

Camera back release

Tele lens slide

Lens

Flash bar socket

Viewfinder

The lens
Focus is normally fixed, so that everything from 4-6 ft to infinity is reasonably sharp, while anything closer will be blurred. On some models you can focus the lens, using symbols that represent subject distance. It is important to keep the lens clean at all times.

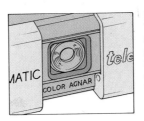

Lens position
The lens is often set inside a square frame, and there may be additional protection for when it is not in use. Built-in close-up and tele lenses slide over the main lens.

Exposure controls
The simplest 110s work best in sunny weather and offer no control over exposures. On models with exposure symbols you can vary the amount of light that the lens lets in to match the weather conditions.

Weather symbols
Symbols – for sun, hazy sun, cloud, and flash – are often used to set exposure.

Flash

With flash you can use your 110 indoors or in dull weather, provided that the subject is no more than 12 ft away. The simplest 110s use a cube that gives four flashes or a bar that gives eight. Electronic flash fits some models, but built-in flash is becoming a standard feature in 110 cameras.

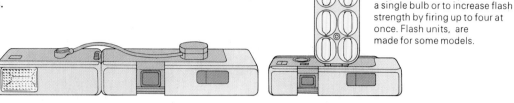

Choosing flash
A bar flash, allows you to fire a single bulb or to increase flash strength by firing up to four at once. Flash units, are made for some models.

Shutter release

Most 110s use a slow shutter speed, and unless you press the release gently you will shake the camera, causing blur. Many recent models have a sensitive shutter release to minimize the problem.

Film types

With 110 cameras you can use black and white negative film, colour transparency film, and both slow and fast colour negative film. All types are supplied in plastic cartridges. Fast (400 ASA) colour negative film allows you to shoot in dull weather, and expands your flash range, but 110s with a built-in filter reduce this film's sensitivity.

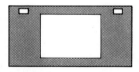

Image size
The small image size of 110 film, above, allows a compact camera design.

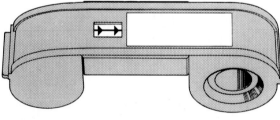

110 cartridge
The sturdy plastic cartridge used for 110 film, left, simply drops into place in the camera. It is just as easy to remove when the film is finished.

Batteries

Cameras that give you a choice of exposures use a light meter powered by batteries. Built-in flash and add-on units also require them. Cameras use one or two 1.5 volt cells, while units take up to four.

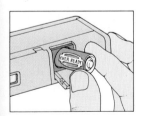

Loading
Before inserting a new battery, left, make sure that the battery and camera terminals are clean. Never leave dead batteries in the camera or flash unit. Insert the battery with the door facing downwards.

126 cameras

110s and 35 mm compact cameras have virtually taken the place of the 126, and only a few models are now made. 126 cameras usually have only one exposure setting and fixed focus between 4 ft and infinity. Some allow exposure control, by means of weather symbols, and focusing, by means of symbols or distances. Most models accept flash cubes, while a few use bars.

DISC CAMERAS

The disc camera forms part of a revolutionary photographic system introduced by Kodak and now being exploited by other manufacturers. Kodak currently sell four models, each no more than 5 ins long, with a height of about 3 ins, and with a pocket-sized thickness of only $\frac{7}{8}$ ins.

The Kodak 4000
Finished in silver and black, this model represents the middle of the price range. Like the 2000, the 6000, and the 8000, it has a fixed-focus lens that gives a sharp image of subjects between 4 ft and infinity. As with the other models, flash is built-in and has a maximum range of 18 ft and a recycling time of just over one second. Its 6V lithium battery is designed to last for five years.

Loading the disc
You open the back of the camera by pulling up a lever and simply dropping in the disc, shown here in its cassette. You can remove the cassette at any time, but you will lose one frame. This facility will be of use when discs with different film speeds become available. You will then be able to change your mind about the sensitivity of the film you are using and substitute another.

The film disc
This exposed and processed disc shows how the negatives are laid out around the central section. When it comes back from the processor with your prints each negative has a number on its reverse. You use the envelope in which the disc is returned to you to indicate the extra copies and enlargements, if any, that you require. There is no need to open the envelope—you just write in the space provided the negative numbers involved.

Disc film
The film itself is the greatest innovation – the camera was designed around it. Fifteen frames of 200 ASA colour negative film surround a $2\frac{1}{2}$ ins-diameter disc, which is contained in a cassette that simply slots into the camera. An integral motor rotates the disc and a pressure plate ensures that each frame is flat, for optimum quality. The negative size – 8 x 10 mm – is even smaller than that of 110 film but the quality of the $4\frac{1}{4}$ x $3\frac{1}{2}$ ins enprints is good, and satisfactory enlargements are possible. The cassette is marked with a serial number, to minimize the risk of mix-ups.

Automatic exposure
All the Kodak models offer completely automatic exposure. They use 1/200 sec at f6 if there is enough light and 1/100 sec at f2.8 with the built-in flash. Three of the cameras switch automatically to flash when light is low, while you make the adjustment yourself with the simplest models.

INSTANT PICTURE CAMERAS

These cameras produce a colour print that develops itself in, depending on the model, from 90 seconds to a few minutes. All models have automatic exposure, and many have built-in flash and automatic focusing. Others have fixed-focus lenses, giving sharpness between a few feet and infinity.

Autofocusing sensor

Lens

Viewfinder

Viewfinder

Lens

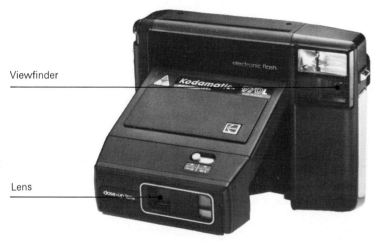

Viewing systems
Most instant picture cameras have a direct vision viewing system in which, despite the name, you look at the scene through a viewfinder that is separate from the lens. A frame in the viewfinder helps you avoid parallax error. One model, however, offers SLR viewing, which means that when you look in the viewfinder you have a view of the subject as the lens sees it.

Flash
Built-in electronic flash is almost universal and is usually of the type that turns itself on and off automatically as required. In one range of cameras the flash is powered by batteries in the film pack. There is one camera with a flash that is linked electronically to the autofocusing system. The unit tilts to light nearby subjects and moves closer to the horizontal the farther away the subject. Several models automatically mix flash with available light, varying the mix according to the lighting conditions.

Film
The cost per print is greater than with ordinary print film, but since you see the result at once you can avoid repeating mistakes and even improve your shots. Film is available in 10-exposure packs, with Kodak (320 ASA) film giving a rectangular picture and Polaroid (600 ASA) film a square image. Always remove the film from its pack by the edges. Don't touch the middle, as this can spoil several prints.

The Kodamatic 970L and the Polaroid 660
Kodak's Kodamatic 970L is a medium-priced model forming part of a range with space-saving folding fronts. It has built-in electronic flash with a maximum coverage of 12 ft. In low light you should use the flash alone, but in sunlight you can use it to fill in shadow areas, provided your subject is within the flash unit's range. The 970L also incorporates a close-up lens which gives you a sharp image of subjects 2–4 ft from the camera. (The normal lens is preset for sharp focus between 4 ft and infinity.) The Polaroid 660 is also medium-priced and is one of a series of cameras designed for use with Polaroid's 600 ASA film. Its sonar autofocusing system is linked to the built-in flash, which provides great accuracy of illumination when flash and natural light are used in combination. In common with other models in the series, the 660 draws power for the flash and for its other functions from batteries in the film pack.

35 mm COMPACT CAMERAS

These cameras fall between 110s and 35 mm SLRs in versatility. Basic compacts have exposure controls in the form of weather symbols, while advanced models offer a range of settings, or automatic exposure. All models have a meter that measures light, to help you (or the camera, if automatic) set the exposure. You focus with a distance or symbol scale, but a growing number of cameras focus automatically.

Shutter release

Frame counter

Lens and controls

Flash cable socket

Hot shoe

Film rewind knob

Viewfinder

Light meter cell

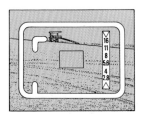

Viewfinder

The viewfinder shows you more than the lens sees. Use the bold white or yellow framing lines or you will lose part of the scene. Many cameras have a light in the viewfinder that tells you when the exposure selected suits the available light. Another common feature is a light which warns you that the required shutter speed is very slow. You risk a blurred picture through camera shake if you hold the camera by hand, so use a tripod or flash.

Film speed control

The sensitivity of 35 mm films varies widely. To match the camera's exposure controls to the speed of the film in use you set a dial on top of the camera or in the lens mount to the film's ASA rating.

Focus and ASA controls
The focusing ring always forms part of the lens and is marked in symbols, right, or distances. The ASA (film speed) dial, right, is often on the lens in 35 mm compact cameras.

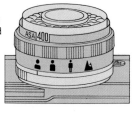

Focus control

The focusing ring on the lens, left, has symbols for close-up (3-6 ft), portrait (6-9 ft), full figure (12 ft), and landscape. With focusing rings marked in distances you must estimate how far away your subject is.

Autofocus

Cameras that focus automatically do so in a split second. Many have an override control that gives you sharp focus on a subject that is not in the centre of the frame. Models using infrared autofocusing can focus in complete darkness. Those working on the image-contrast principle, focus accurately only in the light and provided contrast is good.

Flash

Flash increases the versatility of your compact camera, making it possible to shoot in any light, indoors and outdoors. Most models have a hot shoe to take a flash gun. This synchronizes the action of the gun and the shutter. An increasing number of cameras have built-in flash, giving up to 250 flashes per set of batteries.

Film rewind

When you have finished a film you must wind it back into the cassette before taking it out for processing. (As well as automatically positioning and advancing the film, some models rewind it too.) First, you disengage the film wind-on mechanism, usually by pressing a button on the bottom of the camera. Then you fold out the handle in the rewind knob and, with the camera back facing you, turn it slowly in a clockwise direction. Stop a couple of turns after you feel the film go slack – this means that it has wound back into the cassette. You can now open the camera back, by pulling up the rewind knob, and take out the cassette.

Film

Film for 35 mm compacts comes in three types – for colour prints, black and white prints, and colour transparencies. You can use films with speeds from 25 ASA to 800 ASA, covering a range of lighting conditions, but none of the types of film is available in every speed.

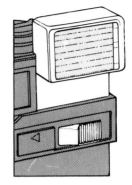

Pop-up flash
Many 35 mm compacts have a built-in unit that lies flush with the camera body when not in use. The flash pops up left, when you press or slide a button, and a light comes on when it is fully charged. The recycling time between flashes varies from model to model, but is not normally less than eight seconds.

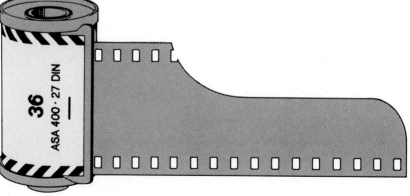

35 mm film
All 35 mm film comes in a metal cassette, right. The image size, above, is good for enlargements.

36
ASA 400 · 27 DIN

Batteries

The light meter in 35 mm compact models is powered by one or more small disc-shaped batteries. The same cells operate the built-in flash in some cameras, while others need separate batteries.

35 mm SLR CAMERAS

The 35 mm SLR, unlike 110 and 35 mm compact cameras, has a viewfinder that lets you see the subject through the lens. You can compose your picture, and check the focus, in the viewfinder. Most models have full-aperture focusing. This means that the selected aperture does not come into effect until you release the shutter, so that you view the scene at maximum brightness, and can compose and focus easily. Nearly all SLRs have a sensitive TTL (through-the-lens) light meter that tells the camera what exposure to set or gives you an accurate idea of what settings to make yourself. Alternative lenses and accessories are available for most models.

Shutter/film speed dial

Film advance lever

Frame counter

Shutter release

Depth of field preview button

Self timer

Hot shoe for flash

Film rewind knob

Aperture ring

Focusing ring

FUJICA

FUJI PHOTO FILM CO.
Lens · Japan
f·55mm
1:2.2
FUJINON

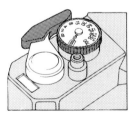

Ease of use
The shutter release should be accessible and with an easy action. A film advance with a short travel lets you wind on rapidly. All figures should be clear. The fastest shutter speed at which you can use electronic flash is often marked in red or with an X.

Camera controls
All 35 mm SLRs have most of the camera controls grouped together on the right side of the camera top. Their position varies slightly between models, and it is important to pick a model with comfortable controls. The shutter speed dial, near right, allows you to set the time for which the shutter stays open during exposure. You normally align the speed you want with a line or dot. The film speed control is normally set on top of the shutter speed dial. By lifting the dial you can turn it until the speed of the film you are using appears in the window. The shutter release, second from right, fires the shutter. Always squeeze it gently. If you stab at it you will shake the camera. To wind on the film after taking a picture, you pull the film advance lever, second from left, right round and then push it back. This also recocks the shutter. You use the frame counter, far left, to keep track of the number of pictures you have taken. When you remove the film, it returns to "o".

Aperture control

The aperture ring allows you to vary the size of the lens opening and so control the amount of light that enters during exposure. It is set behind the focusing ring on the lens.

Aperture ring
This is marked in f numbers, or "stops", left. The lower the f number, the larger the aperture. All lenses use the same scale but maximum and minimum apertures vary between lenses.

Hot shoe and synch socket

Cordless flash guns fit on the hot shoe, but you can use most guns off-camera, for better lighting. You link the gun to a socket on the camera that synchronizes the firing of the shutter with the flash.

Self timer and depth of field preview

The self timer delays the shutter so that you can be in the picture yourself. The depth of field preview shows you how much of the scene will be sharp when the lens stops down to your chosen aperture.

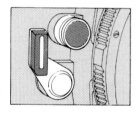

Control positions
The self timer and the depth of field preview, left, are normally close together. The self timer usually allows a delay of up to 15 seconds. The preview button shuts the lens down to the working aperture, darkening the image.

Film rewind

A button beneath the camera disengages the film wind-on. You then use the rewind handle to wind the used film back into the cassette.

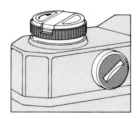

Rewind knob
The handle in the rewind knob, left, pulls out flat for rewinding the film. To open the camera back and release the cassette, you pull the knob up. On some models you have to release a catch as well.

Film

The film choice for SLR cameras is the same as for 35 mm compact models. You can use colour or black and white negative film, or colour transparency film. The range of speeds suits most situations.

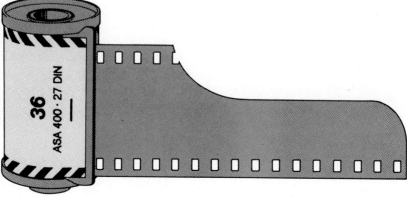

35 mm film
All 35 mm film comes in a metal cassette, right. The image size, above, is good for enlargements.

FILM TYPES

Apart from instant picture film, which requires a special camera, there are three types of film available for your camera, whether it is a 110, a 35 mm compact, or an SLR. The most popular is colour negative film, from which you obtain prints and can make enlargements. Colour transparency film (also known as colour reversal film) gives you a transparent positive which, when mounted in plastic or cardboard, is the slide you show in your projector or viewer. You can obtain prints from transparencies but they are expensive.

Colour transparency film is available in two main forms, to suit different light sources. Daylight film is for use outdoors or with electronic flash or blue flash bulbs. If you use this film under ordinary light bulbs a yellow cast will appear on your pictures. This is very distracting and so tungsten film is available for use in artificial light. Be careful not to use tungsten film outdoors in daylight or it will make everything appear blue.

Black and white negative film has suffered from the popularity of colour prints. Far fewer laboratories process it and 110 owners may even find it hard to buy the film. A new type of black and white film that works in the same way as colour film, and can be processed in the same chemicals, has recently come on the market. While other films are recommended for use at specific speeds, these films, known as chromogenic, produce clear images over a wide range of speeds.

All film packets have important information on the outside. The illustration shows a 35 mm film packet, but the information is similar on 110 cartons. The film format is always given. In this instance it is 135, which denotes 35 mm film. The other formats are given in their most common form, e.g. 110 or 126. The film type—here it is for colour prints, so it is a colour negative film—is also clearly shown. The number of exposures—12, 20, 24, or 36—that you can obtain from the film accompanies the information on the format. The date shown is the date by which the film should be processed. Film is made to reach its best on the dealer's shelf and remain that way for some time. After this, the chemicals in the film begin to deteriorate, so that an out of date film can only give you unsatisfactory results.

The film speed, which indicates how sensitive it is to light, is given in ASA and DIN numbers. The higher the number the "faster", or more sensitive, the film is. On the ASA scale 100 ASA film is four times faster than 25 ASA, while 400 ASA film is roughly three times as fast as 125 ASA film. The faster the film, the less light it needs to record an image, but at the same time a fast film produces a more grainy effect than a slower one.

Films are normally divided into three speed groups. Slow films—up to 100 ASA—need strong light but produce a fine-grained result. Medium films—100–200 ASA—need average light and give medium-grained results. Fast films—400 ASA and above—are useful in poor light, but the grain is noticeable.

Type

Format

Exposures

Process-by date

Speed

Colour film

From colour negative film you can obtain standard prints of roughly $3\frac{1}{2}$ ins × 5 ins. Any number can be made from the negative, although the colour may vary. You can also have enlargements of different sizes made. You can display both 110 and 35 mm colour transparencies with a projector or viewer. You can also obtain prints, but they are costly. Instant picture film gives you the finished print only. Larger laboratories will make reprints for you, but with a rectangular format.

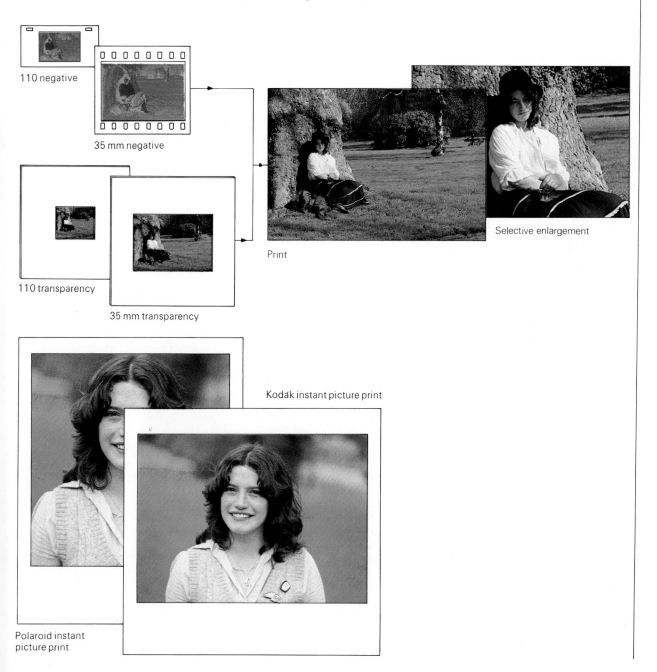

110 negative

35 mm negative

110 transparency

35 mm transparency

Print

Selective enlargement

Kodak instant picture print

Polaroid instant picture print

BLACK AND WHITE FILM

Black and white film is available in negative form only, giving you prints. With slow film – up to 50 ASA – you need a lot of light or a tripod, but the negatives will have a very fine grain and you can obtain sharp enlargements. Medium film – 125 ASA – is suitable when lighting is good. Careful processing will produce only a slight grain and so enlargements can be successful. Fast film – 400 ASA and above – allows you to take pictures in dull or bad weather and at fast moving events, but produces a grainy enlargement.

Slow film

Fast film

Comparative film costs

The chart, right, shows the cost of using the different types of film. Transparency film is relatively cheap, but you need a projector or viewer, and prints from it are expensive. Instant picture film is costly, but you know straight away if the result is what you want.

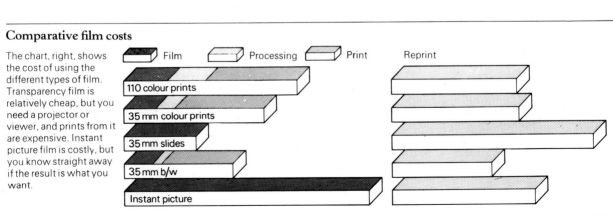

Film   Processing   Print   Reprint

110 colour prints

35 mm colour prints

35 mm slides

35 mm b/w

Instant picture

Choosing black and white film

The film packets shown below represents a selection of readily available black and white films. The type of film you use is largely a matter of personal preference – no one film will meet everybody's needs. Films designed for use over a rangé of ASA speeds are a recent and very useful addition to the black and white market.

Slow film

Ilford Pan F
Speed 50 ASA
Format 35 mm
(20, 36 exposures)

Kodak Panatomic-X
Speed 32 ASA
Format 35 mm
(20, 36 exposures)

Medium film

Boots Panchromatic
Speed 125 ASA
Format 35 mm
(20, 36 exposures)

Ilford FP4
Speed 125 ASA
Format 35 mm
(20, 36 exposures)

Kodak Plus-X
Speed 125 ASA
Format 35 mm
(20, 36 exposures)

Kodak Verichrome
Speed 125 ASA
Format 110 (12
exposures) ; 126 (12,
20 exposures)

Fast film

Chromogenic film

Ilford HP5
Speed 400 ASA
Format 35 mm
(20, 36, 72 exposures)

Kodak Tri-X
Speed 400 ASA
Format 35 mm
(20, 36 exposures)

Ilford XP1
Speed 200–800 ASA
Format 35 mm
(36 exposures)

Agfa Vario XL
Speed 125–1600 ASA
Format 35 mm
(36 exposures)

COLOUR FILM

Whenever possible, buy colour negative or transparency film from a shop with a rapid turnover of stock. A film's colours can deteriorate if it has been on the shelf for a long time or has been stored incorrectly. Avoid unfamiliar brands – you won't go wrong if you stick to the well-known names. It is also important to check the process-by date on the film packet and make sure that you will have enough time to use the whole film before sending it off.

Choosing colour negative film
A selection of readily available colour negative films is shown below. The main factor influencing your choice will be the film speed. As with black and white negative film, the faster the film the less light you need to shoot in. Similarly, the grain in the print becomes more noticeable as film speed increases. You can use all colour negative films in natural or artificial light. The effect of the latter is corrected at the printing stage. The colour characteristics of these films vary slightly, but the differences between brands disappear in the processing and printing.

Medium film

Agfacolor CNS
Speed 80 ASA
Format 110, 126
(12, 20 exposures)
35 mm (12, 20, 36
exposures)

Boots Colourprint 2
Speed 100 ASA
Format 110, 126
(12, 20 exposures)
35 mm (24, 36
exposures)

W H Smith
Speed 100 ASA
Format 110 (24 exp-
osures) ; 126 (24
exposures) ; 35 mm (24,
36 exposures)

Kodacolor II
Speed 100 ASA
Format 110 (12, 24
exposures) ; 126 (12, 20
exposures) ; 35 mm (12,
24, 36 exposures)

Ilford Ilfocolor
Speed 100 ASA
Format 35 mm (24,
36 exposures)

Fast film

Agfacolor CNS 400
Speed 400 ASA
Format 110 (20
exposures) ; 35 mm (24,
36 exposures)

Boots Colourprint 400
Speed 400 ASA
Format 110 (12, 20
exposures) ; 35 mm (24,
36 exposures)

Fujicolor 400
Speed 400 ASA
Format 110 (12, 24
exposures) ; 35 mm
(24, 36 exposures)

Kodacolor 400
Speed 400 ASA
Format 110 (12, 24
exposures) ; 35 mm (12,
24, 36 exposures)

Ilford Ilfocolor
Speed 400 ASA
Format 35 mm (24,
36 exposures)

Choosing colour transparency film

With negative film, inaccurate exposure can be compensated for during printing. Printing does not occur with transparency film, and so exposure in the camera must be very accurate. The colour characteristics of transparency film vary considerably. The descriptions below of popular films indicate where these characteristics are marked.

Slow transparency films give rich colour without grain, but their low sensitivity to light limits their usefulness. Medium films can cope with a wider range of lighting conditions but show more grain. As with high-speed negative films, grain is very noticeable with fast transparency films. Even so, you may prefer a grainy result to not being able to shoot at all in available light.

Check when you buy a film whether the price includes processing. Films that are not process-paid seem like a bargain, but you have to pay about as much again to have them processed. If you use process-paid film don't forget to write your name and address in the box on the envelope provided for its return.

Slow film

Agfacolor CT18
Speed 50 ASA
Format 110, 126 (20 exposures) ; 35 mm (20, 36 exposures). Warm colour. Process-paid.

Boots Colourslide 5
Speed 50 ASA
Format 35 mm (20, 36 exposures).
Process-paid.

Kodak Ektachrome 64
Speed 64 ASA
Format 110 (20 exposures) ; 35 mm (20, 36 exposures). Cool colour. Process extra.

Kodachrome 25
Speed 25 ASA
Format 35 mm (20, 36 exposures).
Process-paid.

Kodachrome 64
Speed 64
Format 110 (20 exposures) ; 35 mm (20, 36 exposures).
Process-paid.

Medium film　　　　　　　　　　　　　　　　　　　　　Fast film

Agfacolor CT21
Speed 100 ASA
Format 35 mm (36 exposures). Warm colour. Process-paid.

Ilfochrome 100
Speed 100 ASA
Format 35 mm (20, 36 exposures).
Process extra.

Agfachrome 200
Speed 200 ASA
Format 35 mm (36 exposures).
Process-paid.

Kodak Ektachrome 200
Speed 200 ASA
Format 35 mm (20, 36 exposures).
Process extra.

Fujichrome 400
Speed 400 ASA
Format 35 mm (20, 36 exposures).
Process-paid.

LOADING THE CAMERA

Loading 110s

Whatever the type of camera you use, it is best to load it in shadow or subdued light. Never open the back in bright sunlight. 110s (and 126s) are the easiest cameras to load – you simply insert the new cartridge and wind on, as shown below.

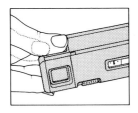 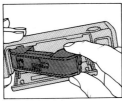 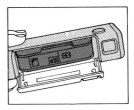 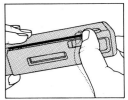

Make sure that the old film is finished and wound on. Then open the camera back, remove the cartridge, and put it somewhere cool.

Insert the large end of the new cartridge in the left side and then push down the other end. There is no need to use force.

When the cartridge is positioned squarely in the camera, close the camera back firmly, making sure that it stays shut.

Wind on until a "1" appears. You may have to fire the shutter several times to do this. The new film is then ready for use.

Loading 35 mm compact and SLR cameras

It takes a little practice to load 35 mm cameras efficiently and quickly. At first you can easily make mistakes and waste film. The pictures show you how to avoid this.

 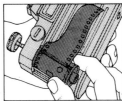 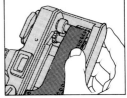 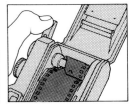

With the camera back towards you, pull up the rewind knob so that the door springs open. Pull the door right back and keep the knob raised.

Put the cassette in the left chamber, with the protruding end facing downwards. Push down the rewind knob and turn it until it clicks into place.

Pull out the film leader and insert it in the slot in the take-up spool. Make sure that the bottom row of perforations engage with the film sprockets.

By firing the shutter and using the film advance lever, wind on the film until both rows of perforations engage with the film sprockets.

Close the camera back and advance the film until a "1" appears in the exposure counter window. Then set the ASA dial to match the film in use.

To unload, push the rewind button and pull out the rewind handle. Turn this clockwise until it goes slack, then open the camera and remove the film.

Automatic loading

On some 35 mm compact and SLR models, film loading is automatic, eliminating the problems caused by misalignment of film and sprockets. With one system, below, you simply insert the cassette and align the leader with marks in the camera. When you close the camera back, the film winds on automatically to the first frame. A red light on the back of the camera tells you the film is correctly loaded and ready for use.

Open the camera back and pull the door right back.

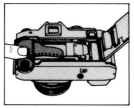

Pull out the film leader and insert the cassette.

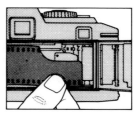

Align the film end with the camera's markings.

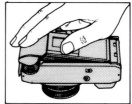

Shut the back. You can shoot when the light shows.

Loading instant picture cameras

Kodak and Polaroid films are packed differently, but you must handle both with care when removing them from the pack. Hold the film by its edges and avoid touching the middle as this can spoil several pictures. See below for loading instructions. You must keep the film rollers clean on all instant picture cameras. On some models they can be taken out for cleaning. When the film is finished, remove it carefully – the pack may have sharp edges. Polaroid packs contain batteries and so should be disposed of straight away – never dismantled.

Loading Kodak film   **Loading Polaroid film**

Remove the yellow wrapping by gently pulling the middle strip in the direction of the arrows.

Insert the thin end, lining up the orange stripe with the orange mark on the camera. Shut the door and release the shutter to eject the cover.

Holding the carton by its edges, open it and carefully tear off the foil sealing strip.

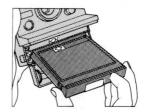

With the coloured tab facing you, push in the pack until the strip breaks open. The cover ejects auto-matically with SX70 film.

ACCESSORIES

Accessories are available for nearly all cameras. Before buying any item, ask yourself: Will it help me take better pictures and will it make difficult subjects easier? Most accessories will, but watch out – the shops are full of unnecessary gadgets as well. The most useful accessories are shown below. Flash guns and filters are also covered in the techniques section.

Flash guns

Electronic flash guns provide a versatile light source for indoor pictures or for short-range outdoor shots. They allow you to shoot in low light, to provide "fill-in" to light the shadows on faces, to freeze movement, and to illuminate small subjects at close range. Unlike the built-in or add-on flash available with 35 mm compacts and 110s, flash guns can be used on or off the camera. Using off-camera flash lets you avoid harsh frontal lighting and give modelling to the face in portraits.

Filters

Filters fit over the lens and change the colour or quality of light reaching the film. You can obtain a wide range of effects with filters for 35 mm cameras. Made of glass or plastic, they screw into the lens. With 110, 126, and instant picture cameras, you normally need to tape a plastic or gelatine filter over the lens. Glass filters are the most expensive but they give the best results. However, each is made to fit one width of lens and if you change lenses you will normally have to buy another filter. System filters overcome this problem – by using different adaptor rings matching the width of your lenses to hold the same filter.

Tripods

If you hold your camera by hand for exposures of longer than 1/60 second you will almost certainly move the camera, however firmly you think you are holding it. The result will be an unsharp picture, or even a blur. If you are planning to get enlargements from your print or project your slides it is even more important to have a sharp image. To hold your camera steady during long exposures or when it is fitted with a heavy lens that throws it out of balance, you should use a tripod. You can use most cameras on a tripod, attaching the tripod to the camera by means of a screw. There are two sizes of tripod screw, so make sure you buy a tripod with the right one for your camera.

The mini tripod, left, is small enough to fit in your pocket when folded. You can use it on any flat surface, and if you hold the camera firmly you can brace the tripod against a wall. A cable release, left, attaches to the shutter release on most 35 mm cameras so that you can shoot without touching the camera. This reduces the risk of camera movement even further.

Lens hoods

When you look into the sun you normally shield your eyes with your hand to cut out the glare. Your lens needs similar protection whenever there is a risk of glare spoiling your picture, and so you fit a hood on it. Lens hoods are used chiefly with 35 mm SLRs, but some are available for compact models. They are made of metal, plastic, or rubber and screw or clip onto the lens. If you use a wide-angle lens, make sure that you get the right hood. Too narrow a hood will produce a circular black border around your picture. A collapsible rubber hood is useful as you can push it flat when you don't need it.

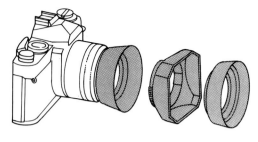

Light meters

All but the most basic cameras have some form of built-in light meter to help you set the right exposure. When your subject is lit from the front with a fairly even light, the meter is usually accurate. But with back-lighting, or a subject that has a wide range of tones, it may be fooled. In such cases it is best to use a hand-held light meter. A cell in the meter measures the intensity of the light reflected from your subject or of the main light source reaching it. You can then read off the appropriate exposure for the film speed you are using.

Motor drives

A motor drive winds on the film automatically and recocks the shutter after each shot. An autowinder is similar, although normally slower. You use a motor drive when you want to take a lot of pictures in quick succession – at a sporting event, for example, or when photographing animals in motion. As you don't have to take your eye from the camera to wind on after each shot, you can be ready for the unexpected. Some cameras, including a few inexpensive 110s, have a built-in motor drive. Most SLRs use the type that fits beneath the camera, giving between two and six frames per second.

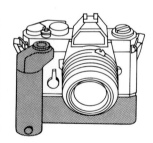

Cases and bags

If your camera was not supplied with a case you should get one. Whatever the cost of the camera, both it and the lens are precision instruments and need protection from damage and dirt. Initially the ever-ready type of camera case, with a drop front, will be adequate, but once you begin to buy accessories or additional lenses you will need a larger container. Reinforced cases give the best protection, but soft shoulder bags are lighter and often cheaper. A case or bag with compartments makes it easier to find things and gives individual protection to your equipment. Resist the temptation to buy a shiny aluminium case. They protect your gear wonderfully but they act like an advertisement to thieves. You can make an inexpensive case from an old suitcase, adding a sheet of foam rubber with spaces cut in it to hold each item and provide added protection.

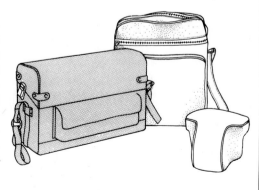

LENSES

Most cameras can be bought with a lens attached, but additional lenses are the most important piece of equipment for expanding the possibilities of your photography. By far the greatest choice is offered by 35 mm SLRs, while a few 35 mm compacts are backed up by a limited range. 110s and instant picture cameras have simple built-in or clip-on lenses. 126 cameras do not have extra lenses.

Additional lenses fall into three broad categories. Close-up, or macro, lenses allow you to focus on subjects very near to the lens. Telephoto lenses act like a telescope. By magnifying the scene they make it possible for you to fill the frame with your subject. Wide-angle lenses have much the same effect as looking through the wrong end of a telescope. They make everything smaller, so that you can get more into your picture.

Lenses for 110 cameras

Many 110 cameras have built-in close-up and telephoto lenses, usually brought into operation by sliding a button on top of the camera. The close-up facility is less easy to use because the viewfinder image does not change when you switch from using the standard lens.

Lenses for instant picture cameras

Only instant picture cameras with SLR viewing offer a choice of lenses. Both close-up and telephoto lenses fit onto the standard lens. The first allows you to focus on subjects as near as 5 ins, while a telephoto attachment, with its large image size, is useful for portraits.

Lenses for SLR cameras

All 35 mm SLR cameras are made for use with interchangeable lenses. In most cases the camera manufacturer offers a range, but you can also buy lenses that are compatible with your model from other makers. The SLR viewing system has the advantage that when you change the lens the view through the viewfinder also changes, so that you can see the effect of the new lens and focus easily with it. When you buy an SLR it may already be fitted with a standard lens, which gives you approximately the same view as your eye.

Lenses are normally classified by their focal length, which determines the magnification of the subject that they give. Focal length is given in millimeters, and the figure for a standard lens on a 35 mm camera is 50 mm or 55 mm. Broadly speaking, wide-angle lenses have a focal length of 35 mm or shorter. A 28 mm lens, illustrated with its effect opposite, is a useful choice as a first wide-angle. Telephoto lenses have a focal length of 85 mm upwards. A medium telephoto of 135 mm is ideal for portraiture. The lens, and its effect, are shown opposite.

Catadioptric lenses, of up to 2000 mm, provide you with extreme focal lengths by reflecting light back and forth along the lens barrel. For this reason they are also known as mirror lenses. They give as long a viewpoint as telephotos, and many are lighter and more compact. They provide a low-cost alternative to expensive long telephoto lenses, being particularly useful if you are interested in sport and nature photography. All catadioptric lenses have a fixed aperture.

28 mm lens

A 28 mm lens gives you a slightly wide-angle view of the scene, above. If you switch to a wide-angle lens from a standard lens, you can get more into the picture without having to change your position in relation to the subject. This type of lens is useful in confined spaces.

50 mm lens

When you use a 50 mm (or 55 mm) lens, the scene appears with a similar degree of magnification to that which your eye gives, above. The relationship of the objects in the picture to each other is also as your eye sees it. A standard lens is useful in a wide range of situations.

135 mm lens

Telephoto lenses of 85 mm to 200 mm are ideal for portraiture. The effect of a 135 mm lens, in the middle of this range, is to give the main subject a generous magnification but to leave enough room for other detail as well. An 85 mm gives less magnification, a 200 mm more.

Convertors for SLR lenses

Various attachments are available that alter a lens's focal length. They range from front-fitting devices that give a wide-angle or even a fisheye effect to teleconvertors that sit between the lens and the camera and increase focal length by two or three times. Image quality may be impaired by these devices and it is certainly best to use one designed specifically for your lens. Other attachments, such as close-up adaptors and reversing rings, increase the lens's magnification, so that you can shoot close up and fill the frame with a sharp image.

ZOOM LENSES

A zoom lens is infinitely adjustable between two focal lengths. By virtue of this, one lens can give you even greater compositional freedom than a bagful of fixed-focal-length lenses. One for one, a zoom lens is nearly always heavier than a fixed-focal-length lens – largely because of the extra glass needed for its construction – but it is bound to be lighter than the two or more lenses it replaces and may well be cheaper. The saving on space is obvious: a zoom lens of, say, 35–70 mm need be no bulkier than either a 35 mm or a 70 mm prime lens.

35–105 mm f3.5/4.5

24–48 mm f3.8

Wide-angle to standard and short-telephoto zooms

There is a steadily growing selection of lenses between 24/28/35 mm and 80/90/105 mm. A lens of, say, 28–80 mm gives you all the benefits of a moderately wide-angle lens, a standard lens, and a short-telephoto lens. A reduced range of 28–50 mm is also very useful, although the extra cost of a 24–48/50 mm may well be justified if you are interested in landscapes or expansive interior shots.

Short-telephoto zooms

Another group of zooms have focal lengths between 70/80 mm and 200/210. (Many just go to 150 mm, though.) A lens that takes you from a viewpoint ideal for portraiture to one that brings medium-range subjects far closer is understandably popular. Prices are often favourable by comparison with lenses incorporating wide-angle focal lengths, as the optical construction is simpler.

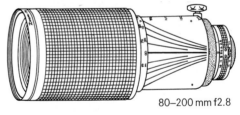

80–200 mm f2.8

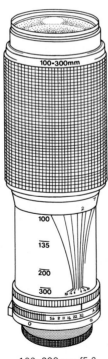

100–300 mm f5.6

Long-telephoto zooms

A third group of lenses have even longer focal length ranges, such as 100–300 mm, 200–600 mm, and right up to 360–1200 mm. The longest of these will pick out fine details at great distance and all will condense the perspective in a landscape to varying degrees, giving an interesting, if unreal, appearance to a scene. The closest focusing distance with very long lenses may be 12 or 13 ft, and so it is very important to focus accurately, as a slight error in your setting may mean you are focused several feet from your subject. Another drawback of ultra-long zooms is that the maximum aperture may be only f8 or even f11.

Macro zooms

Some telephoto zooms offer a macro facility. By switching to the macro setting it is possible to focus as close as $1\frac{1}{2}$ ft in some cases. Telephoto zooms with macro should not be confused with true macro lenses, which are designed to give life-size (1:1) magnification of a subject.

USING YOUR CAMERA

FRAMING AND FOCUSING

Eye position

Depending on the type of camera, the viewfinder either has a frame to show the picture area or is itself equal in size to it. Whatever the type of viewfinder, you will not see the scene as the camera records it unless your eye is properly positioned. To ensure accurate framing, it should be about half an inch from the viewfinder. The pictures below show two of the most common results of wrong eye positioning.

Eye to one side.　　　　Eye too close.

Parallax

Cameras that have the viewfinder separate from the lens can cause the framing problem known as parallax error. The viewfinder shows you a slightly different scene to that covered by the lens, and the difference increases the closer you get to the subject. To avoid losing part of the scene, below left, use the correction marks inside the framing guide with subjects closer than 6 ft.

Correction marks
Cameras in which the viewfinder is separate from the lens produce the framing problem known as parallax error, particularly at close range. Use the inner marks with subjects closer than 10 ft.

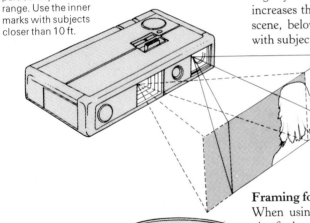

Parallax error
The framing error above is caused by parallax.

Correction marks
Use the correction marks, above, at close range.

Framing for prints

When using print film, leave extra space around the subject in the viewfinder. This is because the printing machines put a 1/10 in mask around the negative to hold it firmly.

Simple focusing systems

Most 110 and 126 cameras, and a few 35 mm compact models, have a fixed-focus lens that is designed to make subjects from about 6 ft to infinity sharp. Everything closer than this will be out of focus. Nearly all compact cameras and all 35 mm SLRs allow you to focus the lens on different subject distances. With many compacts you have to estimate how far away the subject is and then set the distance on a scale on the lens. The scale has subject distances, or symbols that represent distances, or both. More sophisticated compact cameras have coupled-rangefinder focusing. You see a double image in the central portion of the viewfinder until the lens is in focus.

Focusing distances
Focusing distances are shown on the lens barrel, right. Align the distance with a mark on the camera body.

Focusing symbols
Focusing symbols – for close-up (3-6 ft), portrait (6-9 ft), full figure (12 ft), and landscape are marked on the lens barrel, right.

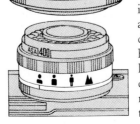

Autofocus

Some 35 mm compact and instant picture cameras focus automatically. You simply aim at the subject and, as you release the shutter, the camera sends out a pulse of sound or light that bounces off the subject and back to the camera. In a split second the camera measures how long the pulse took to return and adjusts the focus accordingly.

Autofocus cameras are not expensive, or difficult to operate, but you must take care when using one. If you are photographing people with a gap between them, the pulse may pass through the middle, so that the camera focuses on the background instead. In such cases, you should focus on the subject, set the camera's focus lock, and then reframe your picture. With landscapes the opposite can occur. If someone or something is between the camera and the view, the pulse will lead the camera to focus too close. Windows and bars also fool the camera, so when you are shooting through a window, or through bars or fences at the zoo, it is best to switch to manual focusing.

Shooting through a fence
In the picture above, the camera focused on the wire mesh in the foreground instead of on the children.

Subjects separated
By passing between the two people, the pulse gave a false distance reading in the shot above.

SLR focusing

35 mm SLRs are the easiest cameras to focus. If what you see in the viewfinder is in focus, then the picture will also be sharp. To help you focus, SLRs have a split-screen aid, below right, that breaks up the image horizontally until it is in focus. Often, there is also a microprism collar surrounding the split screen that remains fuzzy all the while the subject is out of focus.

Focusing ring
To focus, you turn a ring on the lens, right, aligning the subject distance with a mark on the camera.

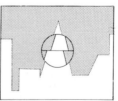

Out of focus   In focus

Focusing with glasses
If you wear glasses you will have problems focusing with an ordinary eyepiece. If you take them off, you can focus for your eye, but the lens will be out of focus. A rubber eyepiece helps, and protects your glasses. Advanced SLRs take corrective eyepieces to suit your sight.

Autofocus in SLRs

Automatic focusing in 35 mm SLRs is relatively new, but some manufacturers already supply an autofocus lens as standard with their camera. True autofocus lenses operate automatically, but with some cameras a built-in autofocus system gives you focusing assistance, normally by means of LEDs, with the range of compatible lenses.

EXPOSURE

All cameras work on the principle of controlling the amount of light that reaches the film's surface. To regulate the light, cameras use two controls – the size of the hole that allows the light to enter the camera (the aperture), and the length of time the hole stays open (the shutter speed). Together, these two controls govern the mix that makes a successful exposure. Too much of either one and your picture will be excessively light (overexposed); too little and it will be excessively dark (underexposed).

On the simplest cameras, both the aperture and shutter speed are fixed. With these cameras, only the speed of the film you select determines the conditions under which you can take a successful picture. Using medium-speed film, for example, you can safely shoot a sunlit subject. But with 400 ASA film, you can shoot in shade, cloud or back light.

If you have a camera with simple controls you can alter the size of the aperture. The choice of apertures is usually indicated by symbols denoting the type of weather. Many 110 and compact cameras now have electric cells for measuring the light intensity. They set the aperture and/or shutter speed automatically. Some also have a light in the viewfinder to indicate if there is sufficient light for a successful picture. Some 35 mm cameras are fully automatic, but most allow you to set either aperture or shutter speeds, or both, from a wide range of options, below.

Aperture control
The aperture control is usually on the lens barrel, and the size of the opening is indicated by f numbers. The lower the number, the larger the aperture. Each successive f number halves the amount of light. Some cameras offer both larger and smaller apertures than those shown.

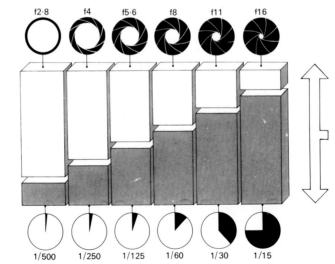

Combining the controls
You combine aperture and shutter speed settings to make an exposure. If you increase the aperture, you can use a shorter shutter speed. If the shutter speed is slow, you can use a correspondingly small aperture.

f2·8   f4   f5·6   f8   f11   f16

1/500   1/250   1/125   1/60   1/30   1/15

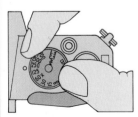

Shutter speed control
The shutter speed control is normally on the top of the camera, and the figures on the dial represent fractions of a second. Each successive speed doubles the amount of time the shutter is open. Some cameras offer both faster and slower speeds than the range shown.

Automatic exposure control

Many 35 mm cameras with built-in light meters are at least semi-automatic. In the type called aperture priority, you set the aperture, and in the shutter priority type you set the shutter speed. In both cases the camera measure the light and sets the other control, taking into consideration the ASA of your film and the settings you have already made. The setting that the camera chooses appears in the viewfinder, right. If the light is too weak or too strong for those settings a warning will show in the viewfinder, and you will have to alter either the aperture or shutter speed until you get a usable combination. If there is insufficient light for any combination, you can use a tripod or flash.

Manual exposure control

Some of the very simplest and some of the most sophisticated 35 mm SLRs have full manual control. You set either the aperture or the shutter speed depending on your subject, and then, using the display in the viewfinder, adjust the other setting until the meter indicates a correct exposure. With the viewfinder, near right, the needle is horizontal when the exposure is correct. In the other viewfinder, a light by the plus sign indicates overexposure, while the lit minus sign means underexposure. When the middle light shows, exposure is correct. Some viewfinders show the settings selected and the film speed in use.

Multimode cameras

Cameras with multimode facilities offer the most versatile control over exposure. Incorporating up to six different exposure systems, they allow you to change from aperture priority to shutter speed priority, or cancel out both modes and use the camera on manual. With a multimode, you can also set the camera for completely automatic exposure. In this mode, the camera will select the best average shutter speed and aperture it can use in the light available. All you have to do is focus the image, compose the picture, and release the shutter. On some models a special mode for flash is also available.

Using the meter

There are three basic meter types: the spot system, which reads exposure from a small central area and works well if the spot area is typical of the scene, the centre-weighted system, which reads light from all over the scene but with increased sensitivity towards the centre, and, most common, the overall or averaging system. Averaging meters assume that any scene contains roughly equal amounts of light areas and dark areas. Obviously, this is not always the case. In a scene with a dark figure against a light background, for example, the averaging meter will make the figure even darker because it does not understand that it is the figure and not the background that is the important element. To overcome this you can take a meter reading from your hand (make sure it is not in shadow), then recompose your picture and shoot. SLRs often allow exposure compensation, while most instant picture cameras have a lighten/darken control. If the scene is lighter than the subject, you can turn this control to lighten. If it is darker than the subject, you turn it the other way.

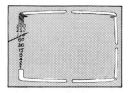

Aperture priority
With this exposure system you set the aperture and the camera sets the shutter speed. This appears in the viewfinder, above.

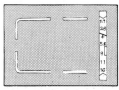

Shutter priority
This system allows you to set the shutter speed, while the camera sets the aperture, showing it in the viewfinder, above.

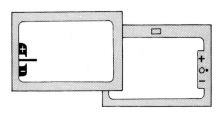

USING EXPOSURE

The correct balance between shutter speed and aperture make for a successful exposure, and this is what the simpler cameras give you automatically. Exposure will normally be a balance between a medium shutter speed (1/60–1/125 second) and a medium aperture (f5.6–f8), and for most subjects this will be adequate. But with a camera that allows you to alter speeds and apertures, your options are much greater.

Manual or semi-automatic cameras will give you a range of shutter speeds from at least 1/500 second to 1 second, plus "B". At "B" the shutter will stay open as long as you keep the shutter release depressed. The top picture, left, was taken using a shutter speed of 1/30 second. At this setting only the static dancer is clearly recorded – the moving figures are very blurred. The bottom picture was taken at 1/500 second, to freeze action. The movement of all the dancers has been completely stopped.

So to "freeze" rapid movement you need to use a fast shutter speed. The speed you select depends entirely on the type of movement, its direction in relation to the camera, and its distance from the camera. Sometimes, though, you will not be able to use a fast shutter speed because the light intensity is not sufficient, even if you use the widest available aperture.

Aperture and depth of field
When you focus, there is always an area in front of and behind the point you are focused on that is also acceptably sharp. This is known as the depth of field and varies in size, becoming deeper as the aperture becomes smaller. Other factors that influence depth of field are your lens's focal length and the subject distance – the nearer your subect is, the shallower the depth of field.

 Large aperture
At f2.8 depth of field is shallow, with only a narrow area in focus.

 Medium aperture
At f8 depth of field is greater, but shutter speed has to be correspondingly slower.

 Small aperture
At f16 depth of field is from near the camera to infinity. Shutter speed is slow.

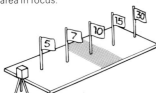

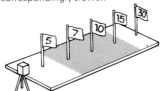

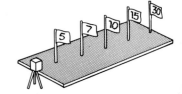

Using shutter speed and aperture

Using different combinations of shutter speed and aperture, you can achieve the same exposure in a variety of ways. As long as each change in shutter speed is matched by a compensating change in aperture you have a large degree of control over depth of field and sharpness, below.

1/500 second at f2.8
This brief shutter speed has stopped even the fastest subject movement. But because of the wide aperture, most of the background is unsharp.

1/60 second at f8
This picture received the same exposure, but with a slower speed and smaller aperture. The bag is now more blurred but the middle area is much sharper.

1/15 second at f16
Here, the same exposure was achieved using a very slow speed and small aperture. Notice that all parts of the figure have blurred with movement, but depth of field extends throughout the frame.

Tips on using exposure

Controlling depth of field

The size of the aperture controls the amount of light entering the camera, and the ring controlling aperture is marked with f numbers. The higher the number, the smaller the aperture, and the greater the depth of field.

Freezing action

The shutter speed controls the length of time for which light entering through the aperture is allowed to act on the film. The shutter speed dial is marked in fractions of a second. The faster the shutter speed, the greater is its action-stopping ability.

Creating blur

If you want to deliberately create blur, to enhance the impression of movement or speed, use a slow shutter speed – 1/60 second or longer. This will not affect static objects if the camera is steady. You will need a tripod unless you are very sure of your hold.

FLASH

When you are shooting indoors, or outdoors on a dull day, flash can provide artificial light so that your pictures will be properly exposed. Some form of flash is available for nearly every camera. All modern 110, 126, and 35 mm compact models take bulb flash, in bar or cube form, and many 110s and compacts have built-in flash. The bars offer eight or ten flashes and with some you can fire several bulbs at once, increasing the lighting range. Cubes give four flashes and rotate as you wind on, so that a new bulb is ready. Magicubes look like other cubes but are not interchangeable with them. They are fired mechanically and are for use with cameras that do not have batteries. All other cubes are fired by a small electric charge from the camera.

Both bars and cubes are tinted blue, to suit daylight colour film. They have a range of about 4 ft to 10 ft, which can be restrictive, particularly outdoors. This type of flash is expensive if you take a lot of pictures; if your camera can take an electronic flash gun it is cheaper in the long run to invest in one.

Magicube
A Magicube, above, is fired mechanically when you release the shutter. Before buying flash cubes, check which type your camera takes.

Flash cube
The flash cube above is fired by batteries in the camera. It has terminals on the bottom for this. You cannot use it with some cameras.

Flipflash
A flipflash, left, is a flash bar that you reverse after using half of the bulbs. It will give you a total of 8-10 flashes.

Electronic flash

The life of an electronic flash tube, whether in a gun, a built-in source, or an add-on unit, is up to 10,000 flashes. This is far more economical than cubes or bars. Electronic flash is available for all cameras. Many 110 and all 35 mm cameras take guns, while an increasing number of 110s and compacts have built-in flash. Add-on units are available for some 110 models. They normally fit on the side of the camera.

Flash guns

A flash gun can cost from a few pounds to over a hundred. Buy the best gun suitable for your camera that you can afford. Its range and recycling time between flashes are both important. Used on the camera's hot shoe, the gun is fired directly. Alternatively, you can use it alongside, or some way from, the camera, with a synchronization cord into the camera's synch socket.

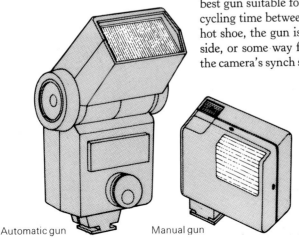

Automatic gun   Manual gun

Choosing a flash gun
Manual flash guns, left, normally have a fixed head for one-directional lighting. A set of batteries will give up to 250 flashes. Automatic guns, far left, adjust flash output to match subject distance. They often have a movable head so that you can bounce flash off flat surfaces.

Using a flash gun

You have to set both the camera's shutter speed and the lens aperture when using a flash gun. The shutter speed is particularly important. If it is too fast the shutter will have opened and closed again before the flash has had time to light the subject fully.

Flash light falls off rapidly, and to expose your subject correctly you must match the aperture setting to the distance the flash light has to travel. Simple guns have a table printed on them that shows you the apertures you require for a range of subject distances.

With other guns you use guide numbers to work out the right aperture. Every gun has a guide number for each type of film used with it. To find the aperture you need, divide the guide number by the flash-to-subject distance (in feet). For example, if the guide number is 110 with 100 ASA film and the subject is 10 ft away, the aperture required is 110 divided by 10, or f11. If the distance had been 20 ft the result would be 5.5, in which case you would set f5.6. As their name suggests, guide numbers provide a guide only. If the subject is in a small, well-lit room you should reduce the aperture by one stop, while in a large, dark room you should increase it by one stop.

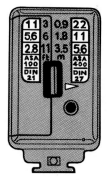

Aperture calculation
Most manual guns show the apertures needed for a range of film speeds and distances. With the gun, left, you would set f2.8 with 100 ASA film and f5.6 with 400 ASA film, with a subject 10 ft away.

Shutter speed
The fastest shutter speed at which you can use flash is usually marked in red or with an "X" on the shutter speed dial. You can use slower speeds, but faster speeds will give partial exposure. If there is a switch with "X" and "M" settings (or two synch sockets marked similarly), you must use the "X" setting for electronic flash ("M" is for bulbs).

Automatic flash guns

Automatic guns have a built-in "computer" and a sensor on the front that measures flash light as it reflects back from the subject. When the subject has received enough light the gun shuts off automatically. With this type of flash you simply set the gun for the aperture that gives you the right overall flash range, set the same aperture on the camera, and shoot. Sophisticated 35 mm cameras take "dedicated" flash that uses the camera's own metering system to control flash output. Exposure information is usually relayed automatically to the viewfinder.

Tips on using flash

●If you use flash cubes, make a note of the type you use.
●Neither Magicubes nor ordinary flash cubes fit all cameras.
●Don't use your flash on subjects outside its range. Taking a picture of a building from across the street, for example, or of a concert from your seat, is a waste of time.
●Increase aperture by one stop, or move closer, at smoky gatherings.
●The flash-ready light on your camera or gun may come on before the flash is fully recharged. Allow a few extra seconds before shooting.
●Avoid pointing the flash towards mirrors, glass, or other highly reflective surfaces. You will get a very distracting glare.
●Double-check the shutter speed on your camera when you are shooting with flash. Pictures where the shutter speed and the flash output were not synchronized are among the most common mistakes.

HANDLING

With all types of camera the most common cause of disappointing pictures is wrong handling. Fingers that get in the way are one of the main problems. They cover the lens and cause black marks; they obscure the light meter and spoil the exposure; they obstruct the print delivery slot on instant picture cameras, causing uneven development; and they cover the built-in flash on 110 and pocket cameras. Your fingers should always be close to the camera controls, so that you can make rapid adjustments.

Camera shake is the other main problem. To most people 1/30 second sounds fast, but for picture taking it is quite slow. For sharp hand-held shots you should use a shutter speed of 1/60 second or faster. Hold the camera firmly in both hands and gently press the shutter release. Never stab at it. If you have to use a shutter speed slower than 1/60 second, you will need to put the camera on a tripod.

Horizontal hold for 35 mm cameras
With the camera parallel to the ground, one hand supports it and the other uses the lens controls, as above.

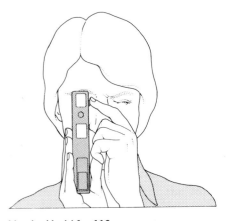

Vertical hold for 110 cameras
Support the camera against the palm of one hand, and release the shutter with the other, above. Try the camera both ways up.

Horizontal hold for 110 cameras
Make sure the camera is horizontal, support it underneath at each end, and keep your fingers away from the front, above.

Standing position
With the feet apart and the elbows in, use either the horizontal or the vertical hold.

Vertical hold for 35 mm cameras
One hand supports the camera, shoots, and winds on, the other uses the lens controls.

Correct stance is also vital. For normal picture taking you should stand with your feet slightly apart, your elbows tucked in, and the camera strap around your neck in case the camera slips or the strap falls in front of the lens. It is best to hold the camera close to your face for extra stability. Variations on this basic stance are shown below.

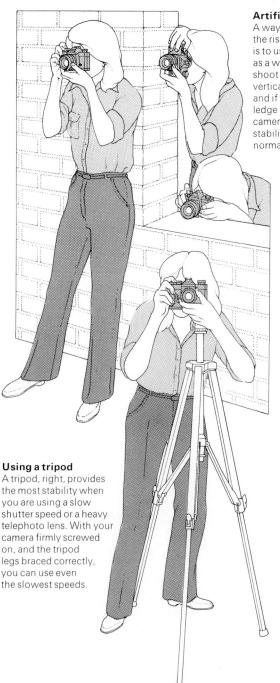

Artificial supports
A way of further reducing the risk of camera shake is to use a support such as a wall, left. You can shoot horizontally or vertically in this position, and if you find a level ledge you can rest the camera on it for greater stability. Don't relax the normal handling rules.

Using a tripod
A tripod, right, provides the most stability when you are using a slow shutter speed or a heavy telephoto lens. With your camera firmly screwed on, and the tripod legs braced correctly, you can use even the slowest speeds.

Sitting position
To get a low viewpoint, you can sit with your elbows on your knees, above.

Lying position
Lying on your stomach, above, has the same advantages as sitting, but is more stable.

Mini tripod
A mini tripod, above, is useful on flat surfaces.

FILTERS

There are two main types of filter. One group corrects the problem of biased colour or contrast. For example, if you use daylight film in artificial light, a blue filter will cut out the yellow cast of the bulbs. The other group creates a range of special effects – subtle, or striking. A diffusing filter, for example, adds a soft, muted effect; a prismatic one produces multiple images, and there is a great range of colour filters – plain, dual-colour, graduated, spot, and so on. Many filters affect

Polarizing filter
The rich blue of the sky, above, was produced by a polarizing filter. Expensive but versatile, a polarizer also makes other colours more brilliant, and reduces or removes the glare from water, glass or other non-metallic reflective surfaces. You rotate it to control its effect.

Colour filters
You can buy colour filters that add one, two – as in the picture, left – or three colour casts. A filter with muted tones gently enhances a scene, while one with bold colours can give a striking effect.

Diffraction filter
A diffraction filter splits strong highlights into spectral colour bursts, above.

Prism filters
There are two main types of prism filter : those that merely multiply the image, and those that also split the light into the colours of the spectrum. A plain prism filter with six facets was used to intensify the bustle and glare of the city at night in the picture, left. Filters with fewer or more facets are also made.

Starburst filters
In the scene below a starburst filter heightened the play of sun on water by creating star-shaped points of light.

exposure. If you do not have TTL metering, you must allow for this (p. 123). Some photographers keep a skylight filter on their lens all the time, to cut out the blue cast of bright light, and protect the lens.

Filters are not usually made for 110, 126, simpler 35 mm compact, or instant picture cameras. This is mainly because the fronts of their lenses are not threaded to accept glass filters. You can get round this problem by buying a push-on filter holder or taping plastic or gelatine filters over the lens. If your camera has a non-TTL light meter, make sure that the filter covers the sensor as well so that it can compensate for any light loss. With a simple, fully automatic camera, you are unlikely to obtain satisfactory results because you will be unable to compensate for exposure.

Glass filters give the best results as they are optically corrected. They need to be handled carefully. You can also use two or more filters, mounted together, for particular effects. You must buy the correct size filter for each individual lens.

A more versatile idea is the plastic filter system, consisting of a variety of interlocking components connected to the camera by a detachable metal ring. If you change to a lens or camera with a different diameter screw thread, you only have to buy a new connecting ring. Although plastic is slightly less satisfactory than glass, the lower cost and wide range of filters makes this system ideal.

COMPOSITION

To a lot of people "composition" has the sound of something they hated at school. All it means in photography is the way you arrange your picture. But it does make the difference between one you like and one you don't. There are no hard-and-fast rules to composition. Just start by asking yourself why you are taking a picture and then make sure that the centre of interest comes over as such.

When people are the main interest, move as close as possible. There is no need to show anyone full-length when all you want to capture is the face. But be aware of your camera's limitations on framing and focusing and do not forget that the processor has to mask the edge of the negative to produce a print. An effective way of concentrating attention on the main subject is to use a ready-made frame, such as overhanging branches or a wall or fence.

A reliable way of emphasizing the importance of your main subject, or subjects, is to apply the rule of thirds. Imagine that your viewfinder is divided into three, both horizontally and vertically. Try and place the main elements of the scene on one of these imaginary lines or where they cross.

The background is often a problem. The best rule is "use it or lose it". Try taking your eye off the main subject and looking all round the

Line
You will improve landscapes if you use the line of a road, fence, or wall to guide the eye into the picture.

Pattern
Repetition need not be boring. The variation in shape between each group of French horns invites attention.

Rule of thirds
The diagram below shows how you should divide a scene in your mind's eye when applying the rule of thirds. Placing twin centres of interest diagonally opposite one another and centred on the intersecting lines, as in the picture, left, uses the full potential of this method of composition.

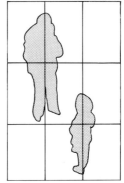

Balance
You risk a dull picture if you ignore the variety of colour, shape and size in most scenes. But it is equally important to balance these differences. In the picture above, strong tone is complemented by neutral tone, horizontal lines are offset by vertical, and square shapes are balanced by rectangular.

viewfinder. Look out for tiny areas of bright colour or other distractions – and for objects that seem to be growing out of people's heads. If the background is still awful you can usually alter your position – different framing often makes a considerable improvement. If this doesn't work, choose a large aperture, to put the background out of focus or use a natural frame to obscure it.

It is useful to indicate scale, particularly with landscapes. A figure, an animal, or other object with a familiar size helps you grasp the scale of the buildings or land formations in your picture.

Never forget that you can turn your camera on its side. Many scenes look better with an upright format, and you will also add variety to your album or slide show.

NATURAL LIGHT

Bright sunlight

You may have to take advantage of bright sunlight with simple cameras or slow film, but it produces dark shadows and very contrasty results. It is good though for shooting dramatic buildings and textured surfaces.

Hazy sunlight

For photographing people, hazy sunlight is far better than bright sunlight. The softer shadows it creates are flattering to faces and your subjects will be able to look into the light without squinting.

Overcast conditions

When the sky is overcast there is little or no shadow and contrast is low. Small areas of bright colour stand out. In the rain light is often soft and colour rich. Shoot in it but keep your camera dry.

Front light

Inexperienced photographers used to be told to keep the sun over their shoulder. The result is often a squinting subject, right. There is little texture and, as the shadows fall behind, little visual interest.

Side light

Side light brings out shadows and texture, giving a scene a three-dimensional look. But it can cause too much contrast. Move around your subject to see how light affects it.

Back light

For silhouettes take an exposure reading from the sky (not the sun). Alternatively, move close to the subject for a reading to give an over-exposed sky. Use a lens hood with direct sun.

Lighting variations

Light is constantly changing. As the time of day and the time of year change, so does its quality, colour, and direction. Photography is about light. By understanding it you will be able to improve your results. The series of pictures below illustrates the changing effect of sunlight. At sunrise, shadows are very long. The angle of the sun makes the light very yellow. Early light often catches high buildings and hilltops leaving the surrounding areas in shadow – a dramatic overall effect. At noon, shadows are short and dark. Pictures exposed for the highlights have black shadows with no detail. In the late afternoon and towards sunset the light is diffuse and the sun a golden or red disc. When measuring for exposure, avoid including the sun. With slide film try shooting one f stop over and one under, as well as exposing "correctly". Work quickly – the sun and clouds seem to change in a very short time.

Early afternoon

Early morning

Late afternoon

Early evening

Winter photography

In snowy weather your camera's exposure meter will overcompensate for the brightness and your subjects will probably be underexposed. Take a light reading from close to the subject or from your own hand, held in front of the lens so that it catches the light in the same way as the subject. Use an ultra-violet filter to cut out the excessive blueness caused by snow.

Lighting quality

The difference between bright sunlight, hazy sunlight, and dull, overcast conditions is obvious even to someone who has never held a camera. But when you take your first pictures, and perhaps for some time while you are learning about the quality of light, you will find your assumptions are too clear-cut and are not really borne out by the results you get with your camera.

Bright sunlight may seem the obvious choice for showing your subject to its best advantage, but it is an uncompromising form of lighting and the harsh shadows it produces often obscure the shape of the subject. Hazy sunlight is frequently far better for bringing out the detail and texture of your subject. The pale, soft-edged shadows that form in such conditions are particularly good for flattering portraits. Bright light diffused through leaves is also good for portraits. It models the face and body in a subtle way, preserving detail by means of soft, weak shadows.

Hazy sunlight
The little girl was captured in hazy sunlight, which served to soften her features and show some definition in her clothing and in the stationary pigeon. The other great advantage of this sort of light is that your subject won't need to squint. If the little girl has her eyes closed here, it is only through excitement.

Bright sunlight
This beach shop was photographed using harsh, midday light. If you have a camera with very simple controls or have only very slow film, you may have to take advantage of this sort of light. You will be able to emphasize bold shapes but will not be able to get a subtle definition of your subject.

Diffused sunlight
In this shot a fairly strong sun reaches the statue through the trees and in doing so is diffused. The shadows are soft enough to allow the form of the figure to be modelled in a way that would not be possible under bright sunlight. The mood is one of tranquillity, which suits the subject well.

PHOTOGRAPHING
THE SUBJECT

PEOPLE

Renowned above all for his pictures of people, Patrick Lichfield took the study of the girl on the opposite page for Me and My Camera.

Patrick, 5th Earl of Lichfield, first held a camera at the age of seven. From using the Vest Pocket Kodak his parents had given him to photograph the dogs and cows on the family estate, he progressed in a very short time to portraits. In October 1962, after Harrow and the Army, he went against his family's wishes by taking up work as a darkroom technician. Called upon to do the occasional shot in the studio, he soon began to attract outside commissions.

The breakthrough came with assignments for prestigious magazines like Life, Look, and Esquire and, eventually, Vogue. Portrait commissions multiplied rapidly. Then came the transition to advertising which, today, absorbs about nine tenths of his time. But Lichfield stays faithful to his earlier interests too. In between advertising work work for, say, an oil giant or a big manufacturing concern, he might fit in a fashion session for a top magazine.

Patrick Lichfield, above, photographing children framed by a window. His assistant holds a reflector to shed light on their faces, so that they stand out from the dark interior.

Lichfield used light from a reflector outside the window to make the study of the girl, right. She is positioned so that the lattice-work in the middle of the window frames her face. The other lattices add interest to the rest of the scene, but do not detract from the main subject.

It is really quite difficult to take good pictures of people you know – pictures that show them looking natural, happy, and recognizably themselves, and express their different moods. For one thing, most people freeze in front of a camera. For another, when you know someone really well it is easy to ignore obvious faults in framing and lighting as you look through your viewfinder – even if these are making the face look quite ugly or unfamiliar – because you see only what you expect to see.

The important thing is to take your time. After you get your camera out, choose a good position to photograph from, organizing people a bit if you have to, set your exposure, and focus (and get your flash ready to fire if you need to use it). Take one or two shots to warm things up, and then wait. People will begin to relax again, and talk to each other, and to you. Meanwhile you will have time to examine your framing more carefully.

Look first at the subject. Are people sitting or standing in natural positions? Are faces clearly visible? Are there any objects in the background apparently growing out of heads? Remember that people themselves make shapes in a picture. Is your subject, or group of subjects, making an attractive shape in the frame? Look around the viewfinder to check the background. Should you move round, to clear it of distracting colours, or move closer, to cut some of it out? When you are happy with the framing, check your focus and exposure settings again, and shoot when people are reacting to each other, or absorbed in an occupation; or speak their name, so that they look up and smile at you. Take several shots in succession, to be sure of a good picture. Expressions change very quickly.

Showing relationships
People looking at the camera appear self-conscious, and unrelated to each other. Try instead to show them responding to each other, in a natural action. The diagonally balanced composition, left, adds a sense of movement to this well timed shot. The family group, above, were lit by daylight from a window, with fill-in flash to remove shadows. When framing a group, try to keep heads at different levels, and arrange people in a clear shape, as in these two pictures.

Daylight is the best light for photographs of people, both indoors and out. But faces look best in very even lighting, without any dark shadows. Try to avoid strong direct sunlight – if people are facing it, they will squint and have "bleached" skin tones, and harsh shadows under the eyes and nose. If they are side-on to it, the contours of the face will be obscured by shadow, and if they have their backs to it, you will only get a dark, featureless blob where the face should be. If the weather is very bright, try to find some open shade to photograph in – but watch for colour casts, such as green light from trees, colours reflected off a painted wall, or blue shadows. A hazy, overcast day is best. Shadows are weak and the light is softer.

You can use a reflector to throw more light on to a face – a white card, white wall, or pale fabric hung over a chair. And on a very sunny day you can use your flash outdoors to fill in the dark shadows. For best results, have your subject's back turned to the sun. You can also use flash to supplement daylight through windows indoors – again placing subjects with their backs to the light, or obliquely, and directing the flash towards their shadowed side. If you diffuse the flash, say with one layer of a white handkerchief draped over it, you will make the effect more natural. If not, your shot may seem to show two "suns".

Most of the millions of pictures taken every year are of families, especially children. When you have young children in the house, it is a good idea to keep your camera loaded with film and close at hand,

Showing character

Expressive background details, characteristic pose, and strong framing all combine in this powerful, humorous shot of a master baker. It was taken with flash "bounced" off the ceiling (see below).

Bouncing flash

You can simulate the light of a hazy day by bouncing your flash off a white wall or ceiling. An automatic gun with a sensor and tilting head will read the correct exposure. For manual control, calculate the flash to subject distance via the ceiling.

because photographic opportunities develop very quickly, and you can't ask children to repeat a natural performance. It is possible to record all the developments and excitement of a child's early years, starting with the birth itself – but you should get permission first before taking any pictures in the hospital. Try to capture all the "firsts" such as smiling, reaching out, baths, solid meals, first steps, and obviously birthdays – up to first day of school, first sight of the sea, and so on. It is sensible if both parents become conversant with the camera, so no chances are missed. Be generous with film, too – if you have an auto-wind camera, use it – a sequence of a child's actions is delightful.

It is very important to choose the right camera position for all your pictures of people, but with children it is especially so. You will get best results if you get down to their level. Seen from an adult's standing height, a child appears fore-shortened. For babies, you may have to lie down flat on the floor, prop them in an armchair, or picture them held in someone's arms. There is no need to include all of the person holding

Babies
Young infants cannot sit unsupported until they are five or six months old. To take pictures, prop the baby on a pillow, as left, or in a baby seat, and get down low so your camera is looking slightly up at the face, so you can see expressions. When they are slightly older, take pictures of meal times in a high chair. The shot, right, was taken in a kitchen by room light. Don't use flash with young babies – they startle easily.

A child's world
When children are absorbed in play, you have time to frame your shots carefully, as in this beautifully composed picture of children playing.

Capturing movement
To freeze the movement of the child on a swing, above, a fast shutter speed and a wide aperture were used.

them. You can get nice shots of a baby looking over the shoulder of someone holding them, too. You will get your best pictures of babies at certain times of day – when they first wake after a sleep, during meals, at bath times, and sometimes when older children are trying to make them smile, or playing with them.

Young children soon forget the camera as they play with toys or friends, or become engrossed in painting, drawing, or the imaginative world of make-believe. This is the time a telephoto lens, or tele facility on your camera comes in useful, as you can stay a little further back to get a natural, characteristic shot. They will probably remain absorbed long enough for you to choose an interesting viewpoint, and take care over framing. Use a shutter speed of at least 1/125 second with children playing, preferably 1/250 second.

For informal portraits, or candid shots, you want to get as close as you can to show expressions clearly. You can take such shots with any camera, but remember its limitations. You may not be able to go closer than 3-4 ft, and this will not quite allow you to fill the frame with someone's head and shoulders. With horizontal framing, you may find it difficult to clear unwanted details from the side of the frame. Try vertical framing, or change your viewpoint so the background is clear, and deliberately include a prop of some kind to balance the shot, like the guitar in the picture shown over. If your camera has a built-in tele lens, or you have a tele adaptor or telephoto lens, you should use it.

Not only will it enable you to fill the frame, but it also gives a much more "natural" look to the shape of a face. Its shallow depth of field also softens distracting backgrounds. And it helps you to put some distance between yourself and the subject, so that they are less conscious of the camera. Don't use a wide-angle lens on faces, unless you want a humorous shot – it distorts facial proportions, exaggerating the subject's nose.

Most people's faces look more attractive from certain angles. Walk around your subject (you can pretend to be checking the background) and talk to them. A face seen in profile, three-quarter view, full face, or looking slightly up or down, can appear quite different in character. The tilt and angle of the head also makes a great deal of difference. So do the shape and position of hands, if they are included.

Fill-in flash
When filling shadows with flash, you want the flash weaker than the daylight, to avoid a "two suns" effect. Diffuse it, or with simple flash stand slightly further back. With a gun, set the camera aperture for the daylight reading but set the gun as if for one f stop larger.

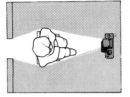

Informal portraits
Try to frame head-and-shoulder shots so they fit neatly in the picture – vertical framing makes this easier. Move around to see whether full face or three-quarter is more attractive and wait for the subject to lift or lower their head, for a characteristic pose. Using shallow depth of field helps to soften backgrounds – focus on the eyes.

Another way of taking natural, candid shots is to shoot from a position where you are unobserved by the subject. This is all right if it is a friend, or member of the family. But strangers, however interesting their faces, may be embarrassed or annoyed if they see you. And they do have some right to privacy. It is usually better to ask first, if you are photographing one person rather than a general scene.

Using props
Picturing a subject with a familiar object such as their guitar can help to show their personality. It can also help you to fill out the frame if your camera will not go closer.

Window portraits
Light falling through a window gives attractive portraits, but will cast shadows on one side of the face. An open book on the table will reflect some light up, and a reflector – white card propped up – will direct light back to the shadowed side.

EVENTS

To illustrate how he records an event, George Hughes covered a wedding. His pictures are shown on this and the opposite page.

Starting out in the early Sixties as a sports photographer, George Hughes soon switched his interest to covering events for a handful of local newspapers. A few years later, the other string to his bow became evident. He joined Practical Photography as a staff writer. Moving on to the busy job of features editor with Amateur Photographer, George still found time to get out with a camera and to write books on the subject. He is currently working on a book with David Bailey. With over 15 years of photographic journalism behind him, George took over recently as editor of What Camera Weekly.

As a photographer, George has two different interests – events and landscape. Each in its own way starts the adrenalin flowing, he says. The difference is, with events you've only got one chance to get it right. Even so, you can make your task easier. First of all, get there early. Find out roughly what will happen and when, and look for the best viewpoints from which to shoot. Try and foresee any obstructions to clear shooting and plan how to get around, or above, them. Never be

After the ceremony, George Hughes takes a shot of the bride, the groom, and the best man, below.

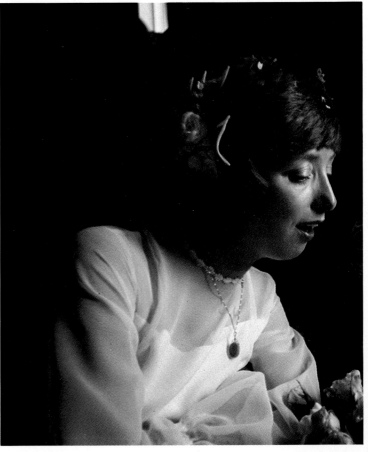

Using natural front lighting, George took this peaceful candid shot of the bride – as valuable for the album as the pictures of the ceremony itself. The confetti still in her hair and the isolated bright colour of the flowers offset the simplicity of the white dress and the all but black background.

without a long lens. If you're on a tight budget, invest in one of the inexpensive zooms now on the market. A 28–90 mm lens, for example, will give you a short telephoto and a slightly wide-angle lens in one. Lastly, don't pass up the chance of any event, however small. You can learn the same lessons whatever the scale.

By framing the bride, groom, and vicar centrally, above, George focused interest on them despite the scale of the church's interior. He could have concentrated on the group by using a long lens or moving nearer, but the viewpoint that he adopted allowed him to include all of the stained-glass window and the structural features of the church, for atmosphere.

The most important event that many cameras get taken to is a wedding. Unless you are very experienced, avoid undertaking the "official" photography – there could be problems if your shots are disappointing. Instead, concentrate on the pictures that the professional won't take – the preparations for the wedding, before he arrives; the celebrations, speeches, and departure of the bride and groom, after he leaves; and the informal portraits and details of gifts, decorations, and catering that recall the day.

While the official photographer is setting up the group photographs, don't shoot over his shoulder – watch and wait until the group relaxes immediately afterwards. Inside the church or registry office, you may not be allowed to use flash. Fast film (and perhaps a mini tripod) should enable you to take some shots. Many churches have galleries which give you a good vantage point (with the vicar's permission).

After the ceremony, you can shoot more freely. Try to get some relaxed pictures of the couple, perhaps in a different setting, like the garden. And watch for the meeting of old friends, or reactions to jokes in speeches, which both make good candid shots.

Some words of warning about receptions, or any other type of party. Take your pictures early on. Later, a smoky atmosphere can absorb over half the light from your flash, and it is easy to get bad pictures once you have had a few drinks. Don't forget the limit of your flash range, and try to diffuse or bounce your flash when photographing people – it is more flattering. If you are taking instant pictures, don't give away the good shots – keep the originals and arrange to send copy prints.

For most large events or shows, indoors or out, choosing a good vantage point is very important. In a theatre, five or six rows back is

Preparations
If you are a member of the immediate family, you can photograph the bride dressing. In the shot above, soft daylight falling through a window, and a filter misted by breath, give a romantic effect.

Candid moments
After the ceremony, people relax. Look out for lively candid shots that capture the spirit of the occasion. Young bridesmaids soon want to play. Wait till one is jumping for joy or running, as here.

Bride and groom
The official photos of the couple will mainly be taken at the front of the church, at the altar and register, and when cutting the cake. Try to capture them more informally, and in different settings. Above, they are framed by the arch as the official photographer takes their picture from inside the church. The departing choir beyond provide visual balance to the composition. Left, a breeze catching the bride's veil as she crosses the garden produces a graceful, gentle mood.

often better than the front row, where the stage may block your view. With a telephoto lens, you can be even further back. For a circus, the front row is best. For an outdoor parade, a first-floor window is usually better than street level. To shoot fireworks, you need a clear space where you can set up a tripod, and give a multiple exposure, as explained below. Hand-held shots are disappointing.

Always check first whether the theater allows you to use flash. If so, you must be within flash range (usually no more than 12 ft) for it to be effective. It is better to rely on the stage lights, which are normally bright enough if you use fast film, and more atmospheric. (Remember to take tungsten light film for slides.) Take care over the exposure. The stage is surrounded by areas of darkness, and this can mislead your camera's meter. Take a reading off the lit area – usually around 1/60 second at f2.8 for 100 ASA film – and override your automatic controls, if necessary, to set that exposure.

To take pictures of events shown on television, you must set a speed of less than 1/30 second (use a tripod). At faster speeds the scanning gun that forms the TV picture will not have time to cover the whole screen, so you will have a black area in your picture. Don't use flash to take this sort of picture. You must not sell shots from your TV screen, for copyright reasons.

Fireworks
For most effective firework pictures, put your camera on a tripod and set the speed to "B" or "T". Use about f8 and, with the lens cap still on, open the shutter. Each time a firework bursts, take the cap off and replace it. Experiment with three or four bursts before winding on. This way you will be able to superimpose several bursts on one frame, but the sky will remain dark.

Street events
Cars and buildings make an ugly background, and crowds obscure your view. A high viewpoint, above, makes the road into the background, while the trees form a frame.

Circus acts

At circuses, a ringside seat is an advantage. You will need a fast shutter speed to capture the action, so make sure you have fast film. You could also shoot at speeds of 1/15 sec or slower, using a mini tripod, to convey the flowing movement of acrobats and trapeze artists. The picture, left, was taken with an 85 mm lens from the front row, on fast tungsten light film.

LANDSCAPE

The Lake District, with some of the best views in Britain, was Derry Brabbs' location for the landscapes below and opposite.

Leeds-based photographer Derry Brabbs, below, on location in the Lake District. He always uses a sturdy tripod and in open country, where a wind can spring up suddenly, it is particularly important to keep the camera steady.

In the picture, right, Derry has created an interesting effect by using a viewpoint that puts Lake Windermere high in the frame. The formation of the trees creates a bowl shape around the lake. The nearer trees and the indistinct appearance of the far bank both emphasize the scale of the scene.

After completing a three-year photography course at Leicester Polytechnic in 1968, Derry Brabbs worked briefly for the TV Times in Manchester and then at the magazine's London office for several years. A period at Yorkshire Television was followed by freelance work in advertising and for books and magazines, during which time Derry shot the pictures for a lavish book on James Herriott's Yorkshire. In 1980 he set up an agency specializing in advertising photography.

Derry sees landscape photography as demanding two complementary skills. By making a fine study of a subject he can plot when lighting conditions will be right. This often means waiting for hours, or even using a compass and map to work out where he should be at a given time to take advantage of the light. Equally, he needs to be ready for surprises. The light may suddenly change dramatically or a slight change of viewpoint may make an unexpected difference.

Tramping around the countryside with a bag full of heavy equipment can dampen anyone's enthusiasm. Derry does allow himself the luxury of a substantial tripod – very necessary in windy conditions – but does not burden himself with too many cameras and lenses. He prefers 28 mm and 200 mm lens but uses a few in between the two extremes. He carries polarizing and graduated filters, but is not interested in the instant "magic" of starburst or multiple-image filters and the like.

When he is using black and white film, Derry keeps a few colour filters with him – yellow or orange, for instance, to contrast sky with clouds. When he works in colour, he uses very slow film, for its rich effect.

The eye is lead into the shot of Grasmere, above, by Derry's inclusion of the pebbles in the foreground. Beyond this the reflections of the cloud and the background hills form a centre of interest. The soft lighting works with the stillness of the water to create tranquillity.

It is so easy to take a quick snap of a beautiful view. Yet the results are normally disappointing: all sense of distance and scale is lost, unwanted details may mar the scene, and either the sky is too pale, or the land too dark. The main reason for this is that your eye sees differently to your camera. Your eye will often not notice ugly or distracting things – even when they are as obvious as a line of pylons – whilst your camera will faithfully record everything in front of it. On the other hand, your eye can range over the whole view, concentrating on some things, and seeing detail in the shadows as well as in the bright clouds. Your other senses are enhancing the view by noticing sounds and smells, and you are aware of distances. But the camera will take in only part of the view, haze may obscure the distance, and detail may be lost.

You must first decide what you want: better snapshots, or landscape photographs. For the former you need to follow some basic rules and use a little care. For the latter you must develop patience and be prepared to wait long hours for the perfect shot. Lenses are more important than at first they seem. A wide-angle lens will get more in. But it will also change the depth of your picture and make objects seem farther away, not just from you but also each other. On the other hand, its greater depth of field will make it easier to get everything in sharp focus, particularly in the foreground, which is very important with

Choosing time of day
This atmospheric picture of the Grand Canyon was taken in the late afternoon. Warm light has brought out the rich reds and purples, and the sun's low, oblique rays cast dramatic shadows revealing three dimensional form and depth. The Grand Canyon is difficult to photograph well – it can look like a flat, painted mural in the wrong lighting.

Conveying depth
The telephoto desert shot, left, uses several devices to convey depth : a foreground object, leading lines giving linear perspective, and aerial perspective.

Averaging
Take one reading with your camera pointed at the sky. Note this down. Take another of the land, with the sky excluded from the frame. Choose an intermediate setting.

landscape pictures. At the other end of the range, a telephoto lens will allow you to concentrate on the detail, whilst its ability to enlarge and "bring forward" distant objects can enhance the drama of a range of hills. The much narrower depth of field must be watched. A telephoto lens is particularly good for emphasizing the effect haze has on distant objects, when each further plane in a landscape appears softer and paler than nearer ones. This effect is called aerial perspective.

It might sound as if it is impossible to photograph landscape with an ordinary camera. This is not the case but, with limited technical help, you have got to be even more careful about how you find and take your pictures. Resist the temptation to take the first picture you see. Stop, think, and above all look. Is it just a pretty view, or will it look better a little way down the path? Is there something that you can include to give scale to the picture? A tree or wall in the foreground, or an animal or person. Perhaps a road with a car winding into the distance, which will lead the eye into the picture. All these things will allow the viewer to grasp the size of things. Perhaps an overhanging tree, or details of grass and flowers, will form a natural frame for your picture. Should you have the horizon low in your picture, to emphasize the sky, or high, to feature the foreground and increase the sense of depth?

Think about the light. Will it be better to wait for the sun to move round a little and change the shadows? Will a gap in the clouds allow the sun to burst through dramatically in a few minutes? These are all things that you must look for if you are going to take good landscape pictures. When you take your exposure reading, remember that sky and land are often very different in brightness. You should do one reading for the sky, and another for the land. Then, if you want some detail in both sky and land, you should pick a setting between the two. This is called "averaging". Preferably you should also bracket your exposures, between the brightest and darkest parts of your picture. This way you not only guarantee a "correct" exposure, but may also discover that a shot exposed to feature the sky strongly (with the land dark), or to feature the land (with the sky white) may be more dramatic.

Showing scale
Including a figure will help to emphasize the scale of a dramatic landscape. But don't let them intrude on their setting. Here, the couple looking into the scene serve to direct your eye to follow their gaze. The overlapping lines of sea and land, and the high horizon, both serve to increase the sense of distance and scale.

Because of the need to show as much detail as possible in landscape photographs, you should use as slow a film as you can. A transparency film such as Kodachrome 25, or a black and white film of 32/50 ASA are ideal. But this slow film speed coupled with your need for depth of field will make a tripod a virtual necessity. With a telephoto lens, you must have a tripod. It is a good idea to carry a string bag that you can fill with stones to make your tripod more stable on windy days. Wind also means that grass and clouds will be moving. You must decide whether you want to stop their motion with a fast shutter speed, remembering that this will cost you depth of field, or let it blur a little, for a sense of movement in your shot.

Filters are very useful with landscape photography, whether you are using colour or black and white. Although most black and white film is panchromatic (sensitive to all colours of light), it records blue lighter

Shape and texture
Try to frame a landscape so that areas of different colour, tone, and texture make clear shapes together. In the shot above, notice how the curve of the hill mirrors the curve of the shore, and the house is placed at the central point, while the variety of textures in trees, clouds and water are clearly contrasted.

Form and line
Simplicity greatly strengthens pictures. Here the photographer concentrated on the sweeping forms and lines of the dunes, excluding everything else. Showing form depends on the way shadows reveal contours to the eye. In bold side lighting, as here, the shadow contours produce strong, graceful lines.

Aerial perspective
Lines of hills in a landscape become progressively paler and bluer with distance, as haze and water in the air between scatter the light. The tops of each ridge are often darker than the valleys between. The effect can be like a stage set of cut-out shapes, as in the shot left. Aerial perspective is emphasized by misty weather, and by long lenses which appear to compress the planes of landscape by enlarging distant parts of it.

than other colours. What you see as a blue sky with fluffy white clouds will look very dull and flat when you get your prints. To correct this you should use a yellow or orange filter over the lens, which will darken the blue and make the clouds stand out more. The rule of thumb for using colour filters with black and white film is that a filter lightens subjects of its own colour, and darkens those of complementary colours. Grey, black, and white are largely unaffected.

A haze or ultraviolet filter is always useful, especially at high altitudes, and also serves to protect your lens. But you should remember to take it off if you want to show aerial perspective and emphasize distance. A polarizing filter is very useful with colour film. It can deepen the blue of the sky, and control reflections. You can also try graduated filters, to darken a sky which is too bright, so that it is nearer in tone to the land, or to put an unnatural colour into the sky.

To improve your landscape photography, it is often helpful to be more selective. What is the most striking feature of the scene you are framing? Is it texture – rippling grass, or a mackerel sky? Is it pattern – a distant plain cut up into fields, or the rhythm of overlapping hills? Is it colour – greenness in spring, or the warm tones of autumn? Is it the wildness of the place – stormy sky, bent and twisted trees, unfarmed moorland? Choose one feature, and see how you can emphasize that and exclude anything else. Simple images convey mood more powerfully than complex ones.

Foreground detail
Filling the foreground with delicate flowers and grasses, so that the view is seen behind them, adds softness and texture and enlivens a rather plain scene.

HOLIDAYS AND TRAVEL

Like Derry Brabbs, I found the Lakes a great stimulation for my travel photographs. I think they capture my feelings about the area.

I bought my first serious camera at the age of 13 and developed my first film – rather badly – a few months later. But for years I was an amateur. One day I called a halt to my first career – in business – put away my balance sheets and became a photographer. I have never been poorer or happier.

I suppose the term "freelance" was originally a medieval word for a mercenary, but it is very apt for photographers. Just as in those days, you have to do what your hirer wants. The art of working freelance is marrying up what you want to do with clients who want the same

I found the disused barn, above, a fascinating setting for a holiday shot of my girlfriend.

By getting her to lean out a little from the balcony, I ensured that Carole caught just enough sunlight to show her face. The close framing benefits her surroundings, bringing out the texture of stone and wood.
The subdued tones of the building are in turn complemented by the blue of the sky, enriched by a polarizing filter.

thing. I don't think of myself as a travel photographer or, for that matter, any other type of photographer. I limit the amount of travel work I do, and I also work for advertising agencies, publishers, designers, and myself. That way, one day I'm shooting in my studio, the next day in, say, Ostend.

Travel photography is about what you feel and notice about a place. London is as much about pints of beer and the pattern of buttons on a Guardsman's tunic as it is about the Houses of Parliament. When you've taken in the broad view, look for the detail as well.

People imagine there's some magic answer in the choice of equipment you use. But there's no right camera, lens, or film. Photography is really about seeing and then transmitting, via your camera, your feelings and impressions to others.

The twilight shot on the shores of Lake Windermere, above, captured the essence of that part of the holiday. It was a very contemplative time and the use of a semi-silhouette helps create this mood. The tree and the gentle sweep of the lake form a soft natural frame for Carole.

Holiday and travel pictures are precious and unrepeatable, so it is worth taking extra care planning your trip to be sure you are not disappointed. Think about what you are going to do with the pictures when you get back. If you are going to take slides, are you going to make up a slide show from them? Are you going to make up an album from your prints? Or are you travelling further afield to an unusual location, and hoping to sell some of your work when you return (see p. 124)? For any trip, it is worth taking some pictures of the packing and preparations, loading the car and setting off, and the stages of the journey and return, as well as shots of the places where you stay, eat, and visit, and people you meet – not forgetting some shots with yourself in. These provide useful links in a slide show or album. Make a rough plan of the kind of pictures you are likely to take, including any more difficult subjects like dim interiors of famous buildings, night

On the road
Shots from a moving vehicle are seldom a success. Your shutter speed may not be fast enough to cut out vibration or freeze the subject, and you have no time to think. It is much better to stop and take a walk to frame the shot properly, as the photographer did for this classic view of the Golden Gate Bridge, taken from a footpath below the main highway. If you do shoot from a car, set the fastest speed you can, avoid touching the side of the car, and take the picture when you are moving towards the subject, so that its apparent motion is least in relation to the camera.

Historic buildings

You can seldom use flash inside churches, museums, or other historic buildings, so you may need to support your camera for a slow exposure. A mini tripod, which you can brace against a pillar, is helpful. For a ceiling, you can lay the camera flat on the floor, pointing up. If you have no cable release, use the self-timer instead to avoid jogging the camera. To take in a large interior, you really need a wide-angle lens, as in the shot of St Peter's in Rome, left. (Notice how the slow shutter speed has caused the moving figures to blur.) Many 35 mm compacts and some 110s have a slightly wide-angle lens, which is useful for indoor subjects.

Famous sites

Postcards can give ideas for effective viewpoints for well known places. Once there, you can explore the subject for an individual approach. Try visiting a site in the early morning, for the fresh sharp light, or in late afternoon when colours turn golden. Here a familiar view of St Mark's Square is transformed by the wind into a pattern of moving flags and birds. If you want to include a person in the shot, place them to one side, or looking into the scene, so they seem part of it – not looking at the camera.

scenes, or close-ups of flowers or locally made crafts, and check off the extra equipment you may need (p. 120).

The main items, apart from your camera and flash, are these: a case (the ever-ready type will do) for your camera, and a lens cap; a comfortable carrying bag, with a shoulder strap, to take flash, accessories and film; spare batteries of the right type, and something to clean the lens. It is also worth taking all the film you will need – it may be more expensive abroad. If you are going to a hot country, you may need a way of keeping your film cool (an insulated bag, and a freezer pack perhaps), and a lens hood is essential. If you intend to take any interior or night shots, a mini tripod is well worth its extra weight, and you should take a cable release (though you can use the camera's self timer to fire the shutter instead).

Before you leave, check that your camera, meter and flash are working, replace batteries, and put fresh film in the camera. If you have bought a new camera, take a test film and check the results, and make sure you understand all the controls. Take any instruction leaflets with you, if you still have them. Make sure your equipment is insured, too. If it is covered by your 'household' policy, let the insurers know that you are taking it on holiday, and check your cover. For new equipment, take receipts with you if you are going abroad in case you get stopped by H.M. Customs on the way back. At airports, people have to go through a metal detector, but luggage is X-rayed. X-rays will damage your film. Keep your camera with you and ask to have film checked by hand. Never leave camera or film anywhere it can get hot, such as the glove compartment or back shelf of your car. Film must be kept cool to preserve its quality.

Local characters

Local people and customs make strong, expressive subjects, and traditional costumes are often rich in colour and design. A telephoto lens may allow you to shoot unobserved and so catch a person in a natural, active moment. (Its shallow depth of field also helps to pick a figure out from the background.) But often it is better simply to go up and ask permission.

Street scenes

The calm waters of a canal street in Venice offset the lively market activity beside it. In the soft afternoon light, the characteristic Venetian architecture is shown finely, in warm, harmonious colours. At midday, the stronger light and shade in narrow streets like these could cause exposure problems (see below).

Light and shade

In narrow streets on sunny days, the mixture of bright sunlight and deep shadow can give you a false exposure reading. Make sure your camera is in the same lighting as the subject. Shoot in shade for a subject on the shady side of the street, as the diagram, right, shows. Move out into the sun for a sunlit subject. Never take shots of a sunny street from a shaded cafe table.

Beach shots
In the middle of the day on a sunny beach, pictures can be disappointing – colours may be bleached and contrast high. Morning and afternoon are better times to shoot. Try to avoid including large areas of featureless sand in a picture. Choose a colourful point of interest, or shoot along the shoreline to include the waves. Here the beach umbrella makes a bold contrast with the neutral background of sand – an effective use of isolated colour.

On the beach, you must protect your camera from salt water and sand. Keep it in its case and in a waterproof, sandproof beach bag when you are not using it. Wipe off any splashes or sand immediately, and keep it in the shade. A skylight or UV filter will protect your lens, and take some of the excess blue out of shots. Beaches are very bright. Here, and in all sunny places – particularly Mediterranean areas in summer – it is usually better to avoid taking pictures in the middle of the day. Contrast will be high, and your eye will see more detail in shadows than the camera will record. With people, it is worth using fill-in flash to reduce shadows. High contrast can also cause you to make exposure errors. These are irremediable if you are shooting slides. For an important shot it is well worth "bracketing" – take one shot at 1 stop over, one at 1 stop under, the metered exposure, for safety.

When you arrive in an area, get a calendar of local events and look at guide books and postcards. These will give you ideas for events and locations for pictures. Always carry your camera with you, and keep your eyes open. The freshness of a foreign setting will awaken your visual awareness as soon as you start looking for subjects. When you are photographing people, whether family or local characters, try to get as close as you can to fill the frame (check your close focusing distance, and remember parallax error). But don't just charge up and start taking pictures. It is discourteous, even offensive in some places. Ask permission – point to your camera if you don't speak the language. Avoid photographing people in military uniforms – you don't want to end up in a police station. You may also be forbidden to photograph near certain military buildings, even in airports, and in some galleries and museums. Always check first.

When you are looking for subjects to capture the flavour of a place, take plenty of details and close-ups: exotic food in a market; unusual

Getting yourself in the picture
All too often, the one person conspicuously absent from holiday pictures is the photographer. It is not always wise to ask a stranger to take a picture. But most modern cameras have a self-timer. Put the camera on a mini-tripod or on a table on some books, and arrange your family for the shot, leaving a space for yourself. Focus and set the exposure, set the timer, and press the shutter. You should have 10 or 12 seconds to join the group.

flowers; characteristic architectural ornament; shop and street signs; clothes outside a store; painted boats; a fisherman's catch laid out on a beach; even washing on a line, or a cat in an alley. Try to fill your viewfinder with colours, patterns, or shapes. Use natural frames like arches, windows, doorways, or natural lead-in lines like a flight of steps or the line of a canal bank, to strengthen overall shots. Shoot in the late afternoon for warm, harmonious colours, or at dusk as the lights come up for atmosphere.

Don't be put off by bad weather. The light can be very soft and beautiful when it is raining, and colours can really glow. Protect your camera in a polythene bag, with the lens poking out of a hole, secured with a rubber band, and a lens hood to keep water off it. Dry the camera thoroughly afterwards.

If you are going on a day trip, make sure you have your camera, accessories, and enough film with you. On such days you may often find yourself in very crowded places – fairs, zoos, famous sites, street markets, annual events. You will have to watch the backgrounds to pictures very carefully for distracting detail. Look around for a good vantage point. If you cannot do it any other way, you can always clear a background by choosing a very low viewpoint and shooting upwards, so the subject is against the sky. In very busy places, you often get your most effective shots at dusk, when some parts of the subject are lost in shadow, and others are silhouetted, and the lights come on to add a warm glow. If you are going to a zoo, do take your telephoto lens if you have one – even borrow one, if you can – because the animals are usually just too far away for successful pictures with a normal lens.

Statues and monuments
A low, close viewpoint, looking up, will make any object seem more imposing. It also has the effect of making the sky into the background, so that the subject is boldly outlined against it – a useful technique for clearing a distracting background in crowded tourist areas.

Fairgrounds
A fast shutter speed has almost frozen the movement of the roundabout swings, silhouetted against the evening sky. The slight blur gives a sense of speed. Early dusk is a good time for fairground pictures – the illuminations come on, providing atmosphere, but there is still enough daylight for hand-held shots.

Look after your film on the way home. The same problems of heat, and X-rays, apply whether film is exposed or not. When you send the film off for processing, don't forget to write your name and address on it. Literally thousands of films are lost this way every year.

With travel pictures, the greatest danger is inertia. "I can't stop the car now", or "I'll come back tomorrow", or "I won't need my camera/flash/tripod today" are remarks that guarantee you will miss a marvellous shot. Take your camera everywhere, and start shooting straight away. Suddenly you will see pictures everywhere.

Close-ups at zoos
Study the movements of zoo animals, and you will often find they have a regular pattern. This will help you to be in the right spot, in advance, for a dramatic close-up shot. The elephant above was photographed with a wide-angle lens giving extra depth of field.

Shots through bars
When bars or wire would spoil a picture, you can sometimes shoot between them – but pay attention to warning notices. Alternatively, you can try setting a wide aperture and/or placing your lens nearer to the bars than its closest focusing distance, so that they will be so out of focus as to virtually vanish.

SPORT AND ACTION

Chris Smith, whose sport and action pictures are in constant demand, took the pictures on these pages for Me and My Camera.

Hartlepool, where most youngsters yield early to the pressure to acquire a "trade", did not hold Chris Smith for long. At 15, as a dark-room boy on a northern paper, he was already storing up the experience that later took him far from the North-East. His first contact with Fleet Street was a fortunate one. Meeting an influential and appreciative

Chris Smith, right, pictured in an ideal position to record the canoeist's battle with the river. Before starting to shoot, Chris worked out the vantage points he would use as the canoe rushed past. The best shots are often the most difficult to manoeuvre in, but it is still essential to keep your balance and hold the camera steady at the same time.

In the shot, above, Chris has caught the canoeist in the thick of the action. Tackling his subject head-on, he can use a slower shutter speed than if the canoe had been travelling at speed across his field of vision. This rule applies whether the subject is moving straight towards the camera or away from it.

picture editor set him on the route he has followed ever since. A clutch of awards – News Photographer of the Year, Photographer of the Year, Sports Photographer of the Year, and others – has in no way made him complacent.

Chris's basic approach was there from the early days. Many young photographers begin work with the minimum of equipment out of necessity. That's Chris's style even now – by choice. But sports photography does demand extra equipment – Chris has to have with him at all sporting events two motor-driven cameras, a spare camera body, and a selection of lenses. His preference for black and white also started early. The medium is ideal for silhouetting figures against an expanse of sky from a low viewpoint – one of his most characteristic tactics. As for composition in general, Chris artlessly puts it down to instinct. But to be fair to others setting out in the same field, instincts are something everyone has, and can be sharpened by experience of the right kind. And that experience is gained by persistence. All sports photography is a question of distilling the events of hours into a few expressive highlights. Inevitably, Chris expends a lot of effort capturing those peaks of action.

By using a zoom lens you can create an exhilarating sense of action, as in the shot, above, even when the subject is moving slowly. Set the lens to its maximum focal length and pre-focus. A focusing screen with a clear centre spot helps you to get the centre of interest – in this case the head – sharp. Using a shutter speed of 1/8 second or slower, zoom back to the other extreme of the lens's range, panning – following the subject with the camera – as you release the shutter.

Action photography is one of the broadest categories for the camera user – it covers any moving subject, from a child playing to a racing event or competitive athletics. When picturing a moving subject, the fundamental decision you have to make is whether to "freeze" it, or to use various kinds of blur to convey its speed. There are two ways of freezing motion: with shutter speed, or with flash. To use flash, you have to be well within flash range – literally only a few feet from the subject with most inexpensive types of flash. The shutter speed that will freeze action depends on the speed of the subject, and its distance and direction of travel in relation to the camera. Subjects travelling directly towards or away from you appear to move slower, and so are easier to freeze, than those travelling across your line of view. Closer subjects appear to move faster than those farther away (you have to weigh this factor against the need to fill your frame).

If your camera has limited, or automatic shutter speed control, freezing action is not easy. Use fast film, so that the camera can set a faster speed. And pick a vantage point where you can capture the action head-on, or at a point where it is slower. Many types of action have a peak, when they slow or halt – that breathless pause at the height of a dancer's leap or an athlete's vault, or at the top of a tennis server's

Peak of action
At the top of his run, a young skateboarder is poised momentarily still, boldly outlined against the sky. It takes careful choice of viewpoint and quick responses to capture such a shot, but you will not need a very fast shutter speed if you time it exactly right.

Panning
Focus on a point ahead
of the subject. Move the
camera back till you have
the subject in the frame.
Then swing your whole
body smoothly and
steadily to hold the
subject still in the frame.
Press the shutter as it
passes the prefocused
point. A tripod with a
panning head helps you
keep the camera level,
and is essential when
panning with a long lens.

Clues to movement
It was fairly easy to
freeze the motion of this
skier, as he was not very
close to the camera, and
was travelling obliquely
to it. He still appears to
be moving, because the
forward slant of his body
and the plume of snow
thrown up by his skis
provide visual clues,
which are emphasized by
the diagonal lines of the
snowfield slopes.

**Shutter speeds for
action (with normal
lens)**
The arrows indicate movement
relative to the camera.

Walking, talking and moving
hands ; slow rivers ; trees
in light wind.

	↔	↕
7-9 ft	1/250 sec	1/125 sec
10-15 ft	1/125 sec	1/60 sec

Running ; children playing ;
swimmers ; horse trotting ;
waves breaking.

	↔	↕
7-9 ft	1/500 sec	1/250 sec
10-15 ft	1/250 sec	1/125 sec

Vehicle or cycle at 30 m.p.h. ;
horse racing ; skiers ; motor-
boats.

	↔	↕
10-15 ft	1/1000 sec	1/500 sec
30 ft	1/500 sec	1/250 sec
60 ft	1/250 sec	1/125 sec

swing. This is the easiest, and often the most dramatic, time to freeze
action. Frozen action appears most convincing if the subject is in mid
air, or in a position impossible for a static object, or if you can see from
a person's face or gesture that they are active, making a great effort, or
excited. A racing car or motor cyclist, if frozen, often merely appears
to be standing still, because there are no clues to its movement.

A low, close viewpoint, which throws a subject against the sky, will
dramatize frozen shots. But allowing part of the subject or background
to blur is often the most effective technique. If you use a slow shutter
speed and swing the camera (following the subject in the frame) as you
press the shutter, the subject will be sharp but the background colours
and shapes will blur into soft streaks. This is called panning, and you

can do it with the simplest camera. If, on the other hand, you keep the camera still, the subject will blur and the background be sharp.

A more serious limitation of pocket, instant, or compact cameras is that you cannot get close enough to the action at many public events. You really need a tele facility. But if you pick more informal, accessible subjects like friends riding or playing tennis, or a local or school sports day, you can find a close enough vantage point. At large events, it is better to take pictures of ancillary details, participants leaving or entering the arena, and so on. A good picture of a muddy but victorious team leaving the field is worth twenty blurred and distant shots.

As with so many areas of photography, it is the 35 mm SLR or advanced rangefinder owner who has the advantage. Of the accessories available in 35 mm, most are useful in action photography. The very long lenses are needed even by press photographers, with their privileged vantage point, to cover field sports. Snooker and other close activities require a wide-angle lens. Winders and motor drives record all the individual stages of an action, and capture the drama of the unexpected spills. Tripods will steady your camera; ultra-fast film allows you to set a fast speed even in bad weather; a zoom lens creates dramatic bursts of movement and colour; a more powerful flash will freeze a graceful high dive; and special effects with prism filters or multiple flash are feasible.

Using blur
This moody shot of a circus rider would be possible with a fairly simple camera. It was shot from a stall, at 1/30 second, with a medium telephoto lens and 400 ASA film. The horse was moving very fast, and colours have blurred into a flurry of movement.

Zoom and pan

A zoom lens remains focused on the same point, as you change its image size. If you zoom back from the furthest extension to the least while your shutter is open, you will get a sharp central point, but with radiating streaks of colour around it. With a moving subject you will also have to pan slightly to hold the subject in the centre of the frame. Set a shutter speed of 1/8 or 1/15 second to give time for the zoom, prefocus with the lens fully extended, and start your pan. Press the shutter and zoom back simultaneously as you reach the prefocused point (it takes a lot of practice). A "one-touch" control zoom is the easiest type to use.

Whatever your equipment, what you need most is a good knowledge of the sport you are photographing. You have to plan in advance to find the camera positions that will give you the best shots – the runner breasting the winning line, the horse and rider falling at a fence, the tennis ace making a wild dive for a difficult return. Your viewpoint should also allow you to set the action against a clear background. This is less important with a telephoto lens, as its shallow depth of field will put backgrounds out of focus. With a telephoto, you must have a tripod, particularly if you are panning with it. You must also increase the shutter speed to freeze action – you may need 1/1000 sec, or faster.

Timing is as important as viewpoint. When you have chosen your location, prefocus on a fixed point, such as a track post, where you want to frame your shot. Set your exposure controls, adjust your tripod if you are using one, and so on, so you are ready to shoot quickly.

Panning with flash

For this technique your flash has to be close enough to the subject to be effective, but your camera may have to be further back, to get all the subject in the frame. Take the flash off camera, with an extension cord, and place it where you want it on a tripod. Determine the daylight exposure, and set about 1/8 second on the camera. Programme the flash to your aperture. Pan the camera, by hand, with the subject, pressing the shutter at a prefocused point and continuing the pan after the flash fires.

PORTRAITS

As an example of his portraiture, Patrick Lichfield offered the expressive study, opposite, of the actor John Mills.

As a photographer of people, Lichfield lays great emphasis on knowing his subjects as thoroughly as he knows the tools of his trade. He's a great talker and storyteller, and this gift is the key to bringing out the expressive quality seen in so many of his portraits. This approach also works for him in fashion and advertising and can't be too highly recommended to anyone seeking those magic moments when the face drops its guard.

But the choice of equipment must feel right too. Lichfield uses lightweight 35 mm SLRs and a medium-format camera. To preview how a shot is going to turn out, he relies heavily on an instant picture camera. He shoots almost exclusively in colour, and is particularly devoted to very slow film, for its excellent colour rendition.

Patrick Lichfield taking a portrait shot. Breaking down the barrier between subject and camera is as important in this type of photography as lighting and composition.

John Mills, opposite, as seen by Lichfield.

A good portrait is more than a good likeness: it should tell you something about the person – their mood, character, and lifestyle. Props and setting can help, but it is the expression and pose of the subject that tell you most, while the lighting and colour scheme control the mood. The successful portrait, the one that looks so spontaneous, is usually the result of painstaking care by the photographer.

The most important thing is to make your subjects relax. Talk to them; play some music; get them to talk to you. Try to photograph people in their own surroundings – sitting in their usual chair, or in their garden. Let children carry a favourite toy, and give people something to do with their hands – a book to read is useful, as it also serves as a reflector. You will work best if you and your subject are alone. Put your camera on a tripod with a long extension release, so that you can come out from behind it. The camera acts as a barrier, and you will only make this worse if you are nervous and fuss around it. You must show confidence, and direct people firmly.

You can improvise most of the equipment you need: a sheet of material will serve as a background: depending on how it is lit, it can be lost in darkness, or richly colourful. White cardboard, paper or sheets of foil will serve as reflectors to direct light into shadows. Indoors, you can use a window light as the main source, if it is bright enough. If you are using flash, take it off the camera, with a synch extension, so you can place it where you want, and tape a torch to it so you can preview its effect. You can use ordinary table or angled lamps, but even with tungsten film results on slides will be very yellow unless you use extra filtering. And they are not very bright. It is better to buy photographic light bulbs, called "photofloods".

The best lens for portraits is a medium telephoto – about 85 mm on a 35 mm camera. A normal lens will do perfectly well, though, as long as you don't go very close, when it may slightly exaggerate nose and chin. Don't use a wide-angle lens, unless you want to caricature a face.

Strong light
Sunlight gives hard shadows, making it difficult to light a face well. But as the bold portrait above shows, the warm colours and sharp facial modelling can effectively convey mood and character. Notice how the subject's sideways position in the chair, and the placing of his hands, produce a diagonal movement in the picture – creating a sense of informality.

Soft daylight
The windblown outdoor portrait, right, suggests character more quietly. Notice how diffuse evening light and a telephoto lens have softened colours. The double portrait on the facing page uses very soft, clear window light, falling away into shadow, to create a delicate, romantic mood. With more than one subject composition is even more important. Notice the placing of the heads, offset and at different levels.

If your camera has a tele slide or converter, use this. Be careful with focusing – concentrate on the eyes.

Posing your subject is the most important part of portraiture. There are no rules: it all depends on the sitter. Ask them to pose however they feel most comfortable, and then check through your viewfinder. Consider carefully what adjustments you need to make to lighting, your own viewpoint, background, and so on. Try to ensure that colours and shapes in the picture – both in the subject, and in the setting – are not taking interest away from the face, and are in tune with the picture's mood. Sometimes, allowing shadow to darken conflicting parts can resolve this problem. When photographing an elderly person, a soft focus filter or nylon stocking over the lens will be gently flattering,

Flash and lens effects
The portrait above was shot using directional flash on a normal lens. The picture, right, was taken with a slightly telephoto lens, by diffused flash off the camera. Both effects are much more flattering. You can diffuse your flash with one layer of a white handkerchief.

softening lines on the face without lessening its character. Don't ask subjects who normally wear glasses to take them off – it would look unnatural. Get them to slowly move their head until you see no reflections from your camera position. If your subject is balding, ask him to look up and lower your camera position; if someone has a double chin, place your camera a little higher. When you are satisfied with your general framing, concentrate on your subject. Ask people to turn and tilt the head, and to shift position, a little at a time, and begin taking pictures as you talk to them.

Expressing a life style
This portrait of an artist in the living room of her remote Welsh cottage is rich in atmosphere and detail. Lit only by dim window light, it was taken handheld on film rated at 800 ASA. The photographer framed the subject herself against a plain wall, so that the emphasis would be mainly on her expression and pose. But he balanced the picture with the contrasting shapes of the dresser and spinning wheel, and the cluttered array of objects which suggest her life, and the passage of time.

HOBBIES AND INTERESTS

Some of the best nature pictures are by Heather Angel. The shots on these pages are the fruit of her patient and expert approach.

Heather Angel is a qualified zoologist and marine biologist. Her first thoughts of photographing nature were triggered off when she took up aqualung diving. Entirely self-taught, she no longer specializes in photographing marine life, but tackles any biological subject, regardless of size. She uses a wide selection of lenses for her 35 mm and medium-format cameras, but enjoys close-up and macrophotography most of all.

During 1979–1980, Heather travelled the length and breadth of the British Isles for her biggest commission — to produce 350 colour transparencies for a major book on the natural history of Britain and Ireland. Coinciding with its publication in summer 1981, Kodak launched an important exhibition of illustrations from the book.

Heather's scientific training stresses the need for accuracy, and she often spends a lot of time in researching sites. While her photographs are taken to convey some point of biological significance, they are by no means straight records, and many have strong artistic appeal. In 1975 she was awarded the Royal Photographic Society's Hood Medal for "her contributions to the advancement of nature photography".

Heather Angel, below, using a survival blanket as a reflector for photographing kingcups in damp woodland.

Heather took the picture, right, in May, as the oak branches were leafing out. A telephoto lens concentrates the eye on a section of the extensive overhead canopy. A special lens for close-up work with small subjects was used for the shot, opposite, of a green-veined white butterfly resting on a crosswort flower. Natural light from behind defines the body and wings and separates the butterfly from the background.

One of the most enjoyable ways to use your photography is in conjunction with other interests. But whether you are a nature lover, a keen gardener, an expert modelmaker, or a stamp collector, you will soon find that you need to acquire additional skills and items of equipment to photograph your subjects. A naturalist or birdwatcher may want a telephoto lens, or access to a hide. An aquarium owner needs to construct a set-up to photograph his fish. Pictures of flowers involve using windshields, reflectors, and a tripod. And for most hobbies, you will want to take pictures closer than your normal lens can focus.

Close-up attachments are available for many cameras. One or two 110 models have a built-in close-up or "macro" facility, and others take a close-up fitting. For 35 mm compacts, you may be able to use supplementary close-up lenses, of different strengths, which screw on to your main lens like filters. None of these devices is very powerful. And without TTL (through-the-lens) viewing, you will have to measure the lens-to-subject distance exactly with a tape or ruler, to be sure of sharp focus. With a 35 mm SLR your choice is wide. You can again use supplementary lenses, or you can buy a set of extension tubes which fit between the camera and lens. These are quite powerful, and not very expensive; but unless you buy automatic tubes designed for your camera, the auto aperture control of your lens will be uncoupled, so that the aperture closes down as you adjust it, darkening the image. The most versatile, but costly, close-up device is a macro lens. This

Aquarium shots
Clean the front glass of your tank thoroughly and slide a sheet of glass into it to limit the movements of the fish. Place a piece of black card against the front (and back if it has no backing), and cut a hole in it for your lens. Set up the camera and flash as shown, placing the gun on a stand so it fires at a 45 degree angle to the water surface. Use a torch taped to the flash to check that there will be no distracting reflections.

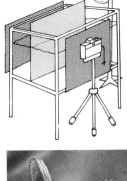

Flower pictures
To get good pictures of flowers you need a close-up attachment or macro lens, a tripod, and a windshield to stop the flowers moving. This can double as a plain background, to pick out a few blooms, as in the picture right. Daylight, with a reflector to fill shadows, will give the most natural lighting. Set as small an aperture as possible, and focus very carefully.

Choosing nature subjects

If you have only a normal lens, it is not worth trying to take pictures of tiny close-up flowers, or distant birds. You can fill your frame more effectively with the forms, textures, and colours of the natural world. Don't restrict yourself to shots from eye – level – point your camera directly up, for shots of a woodland canopy against the sky, or down for the tangled undergrowth of the woodland floor. And look for the striking forms of gnarled roots and boughs, or the delicate patterns of young leaves, translucent with the light behind.

couples to your camera like any other lens, so that you can use focusing and exposure controls normally, but can focus to within a few inches. It gives fine, pin-sharp images up to almost life size, and can also be used as an ordinary lens – a 50 mm macro replaces a standard lens.

But you need more than good close-up equipment to take successful pictures of small subjects. In close-up shots, depth of field is very limited, while the slightest subject or camera movement will cause blur. You will need a tripod and release, to keep the camera still and allow you to set a longer exposure and so reduce aperture, to increase depth of field. For flowers and plants, in your garden or in the country-side, you will also need a windshield, to stop them moving. This can double as a plain background, to isolate one or two blooms from their surroundings. If you place it a few inches back, it will be out of focus and appear as merely a soft colour behind the subject. A white wind-shield, placed out of frame, can also serve as a reflector, to throw more light on the flower and fill in shadows. Try to use daylight, not flash, as colours and forms will appear more natural. Another useful tip with flowers is to use a weak filter of the same colour as the petals to strengthen the colour of the bloom in your picture. This is particularly helpful with pale flowers, that might "bleach out" with the slightest error in exposure.

Most forms of close-up photography involve the same problems – isolating the subject from a distracting background, lighting it evenly,

Showing small objects

If you have no close-up facility, group a number of small items together on a dark, contrasting background and arrange them to fill the area your lens can take in and show sharply. This shot was taken with a slightly wide-angle lens. Keep the lighting even, and set a small aperture, for depth of field, focusing very carefully. It is best to use a tripod.

Without a close-up lens or attachment, you cannot photograph small models in fine detail. One solution is to include the model maker in the shot, to show his skill. Shooting from above will show the model clearly, and the hands, but not the face. From the front the hands may partly obscure the model. Try a side view, as in the picture, left. You may also find it useful to adopt a slightly higher viewpoint, looking down onto the work in progress.

and getting enough depth of field. Set models or other small items on a plain, contrasting background. If you are using flash, or lamps, place reflectors round the subject to spread the light evenly. If a model is a little in front of the background, you can either light the background separately with a small lamp, to bring up its colour, or leave it to go dark. Rather than trying to calculate a close-up flash exposure, take the gun off the camera, using an extension cord, and set it up on a tripod further back, with a torch taped to it to show how its light will fall. It is the distance of the flash from the subject that determines the exposure, not the camera. If you are photographing glass, or china ornaments, you will find it easier to see how reflections will fall using photolamps (with tungsten film, for slides), not flash.

With birds, a table or feeder in your garden will give you a regular flow of subjects. But you still cannot get very close. If you have a telephoto lens, you can set it on a tripod some distance away from the birds. But you may find you have not got enough speed to freeze their action except on very sunny days. Try mounting your flash gun near the bird table, at the distance that gives the smallest aperture. Connect the flash to your camera with a flash extension cord. Set the flash aperture on your camera, however far the camera is away, and set the shutter for flash. Use slow film so that exposure settings suit the available daylight. If you haven't got a telephoto lens, you can mount the camera and flash together on a tripod and use a long air (or bulb) release on the camera.

Be prepared to do research, to experiment, and to be patient. You will be rewarded with better pictures, the result of hours of enjoyment.

Simulated backgrounds
Pictures of your models may look more effective against painted backgrounds or photographs of real settings. You could also project a slide on to a screen, and set the model up in front, separately lit. It is often helpful to light the model and its background separately, placing them a little apart (not too far, or limited depth of field will put the background, or the model, out of focus). This avoids shadows cast by the subject appearing on the background.

DOCUMENTARY

Me and My Camera sent Homer Sykes to Saltaire, in Yorkshire, to shoot the examples below and opposite of documentary photography.

Homer Sykes has long known the value of melting into the background and waiting for the opportunity for a picture to arise. As a teenager, he haunted the out-of-the-way places that yielded the subjects he still pursues – ordinary people in their environment. The relationship of people to where they live, work, and play – so clear to see but so often ignored – is of the essence in his pictures. A book of his photographs of British country customs was the first major fruit of this fascination. Homer's initial involvement with the subject was through a project he

A brief moment in Homer Sykes' documentation of life in Saltaire, Yorkshire, above. This is the material of which unbiased pictorial records are made.

The closeness of the country to urban life comes across in Homer's shot, right. Returning home from work tired, the man is only a little way from the woods and fields. Yet he seems to be held in by the railway, the fence, the heavy pattern of the cobbled street, and the tall natural frames either side of him.

was carrying out at college. Once the idea of the book seized him, he spent four years shooting, researching and writing to produce it.

Homer likes above all to travel light, taking with him a Leica rangefinder, a standard 50 mm lens, and some black and white film. The demands of earning a living as a Press photographer more often than not burden him with far more equipment, but many of his published pictures do represent a marriage between his own interests and what the public wants to see. The fact that his work has been featured prominently in the Daily Mirror as well as in more sober publications demonstrates this.

Documentary photography need not be as dry as it sounds. As Homer demonstrates, it is a question of feeling as much as any other branch of photography. His pictures not only tell you about the lives of his subjects – they tell you how he feels about what he sees. The situations he wants to photograph don't come to order. Since this is the case, Homer – like anyone else wanting to create a photographic record – can never afford to be without a camera and a supply of film.

With the natural light shot, above, Homer shows the value of finding a subject who is oblivious of the camera. The woman's absorption in her work is really the subject. Her exertions are in contrast to the ordered rows of cotton spools behind her. Objects like this are inseparable in documentary shots from the people in whose lives they play an everyday part.

Why take pictures of where you live and work, or of the environment and lives of others? Times and places are continually altering – buildings are pulled down, old crafts and work patterns die out, design styles come and go. Our cities, towns, and countryside present a varied and ever-changing face. These pictures of New York show how the camera can record, in a single day, four quite different aspects of a city's character. Using your camera to record the world can be immensely rewarding. You may pursue a special interest in one subject – street markets say, or canal boats and their owners. Or you may want to record a local area, an event, or a style of architecture. Or you may simply want to observe and record your own environment for your grandchildren to see.

Night life
At night, when the neon lights come on, streets are full of life and all distracting or jarring details are lost in shadow. Try shooting at dusk, as below. There will still be some colour in the sky and detail in the buildings.

Modern architecture
The stark, geometric forms of a cluster of New York's modern skyscrapers are emphasized by brilliant, hard side-lighting, with sharp edged shadows. Notice how the low viewpoint makes the buildings taper strongly, emphasizing their height.

Street colour
New York is a city made up of many cities, a melting pot of cultures. This shot, left, of an Italian street restaurant captures a striking mixture of Mediterranean and American styles.

The classic view
The Empire State Building symbolizes New York's aspiring culture. Seen from the canyon-like streets below it can be unimpressive. But here, photographed from a high viewpoint on another tower building, it stands out boldly against the panorama of the city lying in the late afternoon sun.

In documenting a subject, look for a balance of large scale shots and detail, environment and people, single faces and street scenes. There is no "right equipment" for this kind of photography – but remember that you will have to carry everything with you, and you will often be shooting by "available" light, to capture atmosphere – daylight, street lights at night, tungsten or neon or fluorescent light indoors. You may want to use black and white film, because it avoids problems of colour balance and is far more versatile in dim light. You can set your camera to double, or double again, the quoted ASA speed of the film, to improve shutter speed for handheld pictures without flash. (This is called "uprating" or "pushing" your film. Tell the processor what you have done, and don't change ASA in mid-film. Alternatively you can use the new "chromogenic" black and white films, that allow variable ASA settings on one film from 125 ASA to 1600 ASA.) Black and white photography also helps to simplify complex, distracting backgrounds, and by its association with news shots, suggests a realistic mood.

When photographing people at work, ask permission of the employers first. Avoid flash if possible, and people will soon forget you are around. Try to capture all the stages and detail of their work, and the skills involved. Get some shots which show their hands and face clearly, expressing concentration, and others that emphasize the work or project itself, and the work place. For candid shots, the SLR is rather noisy. Use a quiet camera. Measure exposure (say from your hand) away from people and also prefocus – say at about 12 ft at f8. You can take pictures of anyone in a public place like a street, but you cannot necessarily publish or display them if it could cause offence.

Showing a skill
People at work will often be looking down, concentrating on the task. You will need a fairly low view to capture their expression, and relate it to the centre of their attention, their hands and the object they are working on. The two pictures on this page are of a craftsman making a wheel for a traditional cart, a skill that is now dying out in rural places.

Showing a project
The shot right is one of a series showing the assembly of the wheel. A wide-angle lens almost fills the foreground with the bold, curving shape.

APPENDICES

PRINT PRESENTATION

When you have looked at your prints, you should sort them out. Throw or give away duplicates, and discard any that have not worked. Store the others in an album. This makes them easier to look at, and helps preserve them. Buy ready-made frames or perspex cubes for wall or table display. A good alternative to frames are wall-blocks of chipboard with an adhesive surface. They make print-mounting easy and, like frames, come in a range of sizes.

Making a cut-out mount

One of the simplest ways of presenting your prints is a cut-out mount, right. Take a piece of card stiff enough to stand up but not too thick to bend neatly, and fold it in half horizontally. Cut diagonal slits in the front of the card to create a glueless frame for your print. We have shown here an instant picture print, but you can just as easily cut diagonals to suit horizontal- or vertical-format 110 or 35 mm enprints. For a more permanent display, stick the print on a piece of block-board. Varnish the board's edges for a more finished look.

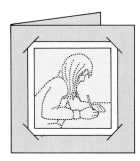

Masking a print

A mask or "mat" allows you to hide unwanted parts of the picture, and it provides a pleasing border. You need a piece of card the same size as your picture frame.

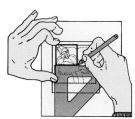

Tracing the print
Trace the area you want to show. Use the tracing to mark the card.

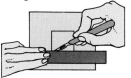

Cutting the card
Cut out the resulting square or rectangle from the centre of the card.

Framing prints

Even a simple frame makes your prints look more impressive when you hang them on the wall. The frame, right, is easy to make. Using metal clips, you clamp your prints between sheets of glass and hardboard. Alternatively, you can buy kits containing a metal or wooden frame.

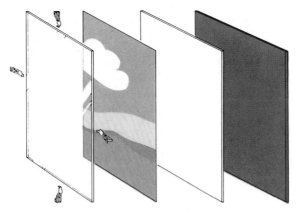

Using an album

An album provides protection for your prints. Some albums have clear plastic overlays ; others take plastic sleeves. Corner mounts are also available, while rubber cement, dry mounting, and pages with slit corners provide other methods.

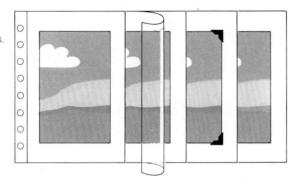

Ordering reprints

If you want to re-order prints or enlargements, take the print as well as the negative to the shop, so that there is no doubt about which one you want. A reprint will be the same size as your enprint. Because of printing methods, the reprint will probably differ slightly in colour from your original print. But if the colours seem too different, you should ask for the print to be done again. Look at the prints before leaving the shop, to make sure you have what you want.

Enlargements

With 110 prints you must have the whole picture enlarged. With other formats you can select an area for enlargement. But because most enlargements are made on machines, the amount of choice you have is limited. You can ask for hand-made enlargements, but these are expensive. It is usually cheaper to order a machine-made enlargement and make a mask before you frame it.

Other uses for your prints

You can use your pictures as Christmas and greetings cards. Many processors offer special Christmas folders. These are more personal, and can be cheaper than regular cards. Another possibility is to use one of your pictures as a change of address card. A shot of your family and new home is ideal for this purpose.

Handling negatives
Always handle your negatives with extreme care. Unlike prints, they are impossible to replace once damaged. Hold them by the edges, and never touch the surface of the image. Protect them from dust and abrasions by keeping them in the clear plastic or paper containers supplied by the processing lab.

SLIDE PRESENTATION

Most slides are returned from the processor, ready mounted, in plastic boxes just large enough to hold one film. You can also buy wooden, metal or plastic storage boxes that accommodate several hundred slides. A much better storage system, which allows you to see a selection of slides at one time, uses plastic wallets with pockets to hold 36 mounted slides. You can keep the wallets either in a ring-back folder or suspended in a metal filing cabinet.

Whichever system you use, make sure your slides are kept cool and dry. Moisture in the air encourages fungus.

Slide mounts
Mounts are usually plastic or self-adhesive cardboard, right. Glass-fronted mounts are better for protecting slides.

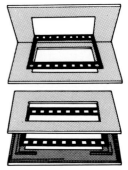

Viewers and projectors
Slide viewers are either mains or battery operated. They have a magnifying lens and can be used in daylight, for display or for previewing slides for projection. Slide projectors are available in a variety of designs, and they are the only practical method of showing your work to a number of people. Some types take interchangeable and zoom lenses.

Viewers
A diffused lamp inside provides illumination for the slide.

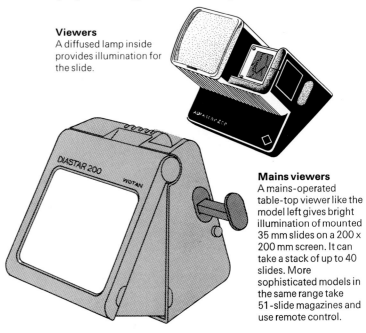

Mains viewers
A mains-operated table-top viewer like the model left gives bright illumination of mounted 35 mm slides on a 200 x 200 mm screen. It can take a stack of up to 40 slides. More sophisticated models in the same range take 51-slide magazines and use remote control.

Projectors

Most projectors align and display the slides automatically. You simply change the slide in view by pressing a button. They have forwards and backwards control, usually by means of a remote control panel. Advanced types, right, feature automatic focusing. You usually have a choice between straight magazines holding up to 80 slides, right, and circular magazines, below, holding about 100 slides.

Manual projectors

With these projectors, you load slides individually into the carrier and then push them in front of the lamp. Some models eject the previous slide, but others have to be unloaded by hand as well.

Projection screens

You can use any flat, white wall as a projection surface. But, for best results, you need a purpose-built screen. There are two main types of screen surface – matte and beaded. For small rooms, a matte screen is best. The image is less bright than with some others, but the screen can be viewed from all angles. Use a beaded screen in rooms that you cannot completely black out. The surface throws back a very brilliant image, but has quite a narrow reflective angle, so you must sit closer to the projector to see a distortion-free picture.

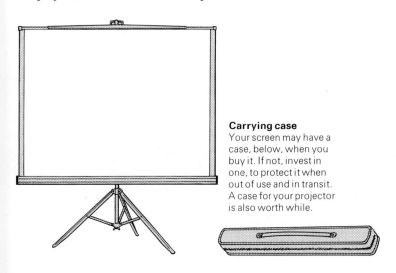

Carrying case

Your screen may have a case, below, when you buy it. If not, invest in one, to protect it when out of use and in transit. A case for your projector is also worth while.

Preparing a slide show

Careful preparation of your slides ensures a successful show. Edit your slides ruthlessly so that only the very best and the most relevant are left. If you are in any doubt about a particular shot, the best policy is to leave it out. Use your viewer or projector to preview the slides, and if you want to give a commentary during the show, make clear and comprehensive notes on them. The story element of a successful slide show is often important, so use any detail shots you may have of maps, place names or souvenirs – they all help to give interest and authenticity. Don't leave any slide in the projector for more than a few seconds, and limit the show to about 20–25 minutes.

To keep slides the right way round for projection, mark a spot on the bottom left-hand corner of the front of the mount. Load the slide with the spot top right, facing the back of the magazine. After final selection, draw a diagonal line with a felt-tipped pen across the tops of the mounts to keep them in order, below.

Selecting slides

As an aid to selecting slides, a light box is ideal. It consists of an evenly lit white surface (usually glass, but sometimes plastic), on which you can place a large selection of slides. To save money, you can make your own by supporting a piece of glass or plastic over white paper lit by a lamp below the glass, right.

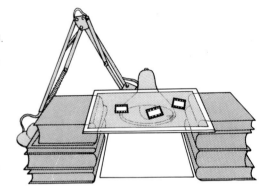

Captioning slides

The more films you take the more difficult it becomes to remember details about the images. As an aid to memory, write relevant information, such as date and location, directly on to cardboard mounts, or on sticky labels for plastic mounts.

Ordering slides

Use a diagonal line, left, to keep slides in order, and a spot, right, to help load the magazine.

CAMERA CARE

Looking after your camera not only prolongs its working life, but also ensures that your pictures don't suffer needlessly. It is easy for dust and bits of lint to enter the camera and cause spots on your pictures, make the shutter inaccurate, or even jam it, so don't open the back unless you have to. Bits of film, torn off by damaged sprockets, can also jam 35 mm cameras. Avoid touching the lens with your fingers. Smears will ruin your pictures and the weak acid in your skin can harm the surface. Cleaning is easy, but don't push at the shutter blind on any 35 mm camera or touch the mirror on SLRs. Keep the outside of the camera clean, to reduce the amount of dust that gets inside. If your camera becomes very dirty, take it to a reputable repairer for cleaning and checking. Your dealer will usually be able to recommend one.

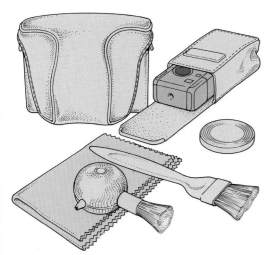

Cleaning kit
A few inexpensive items, left, are all you need to keep your camera and lens clean. You should have a blower brush, a camel hair brush and a soft paint brush, and an antistatic lens cloth. Leave the lens cap on when the camera is not in use and store the camera in a case with a pack of silica gel. Keep this away from children.

Cleaning the lens
Use the blower brush or the ordinary brush to remove dust, then use the cloth in a gentle, clockwise motion.

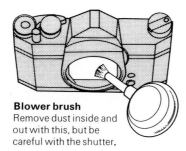

Blower brush
Remove dust inside and out with this, but be careful with the shutter.

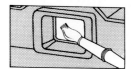

Cleaning the viewfinder
To clean in the corners of the viewfinder and other difficult spots, use the paint brush.

CAMERA FAULTS

Some camera faults you can detect before you press the shutter. The illustrations below show the main things you should check. The pages on Picture faults will also help you if results are unsatisfactory. If these checks draw a blank, claim on the guarantee or use a reliable repairer.

Pocket cameras

If the shutter will not press, it could be for any of the reasons shown below. If problems persist, don't try to repair the camera yourself, but take it to a reputable repair shop.

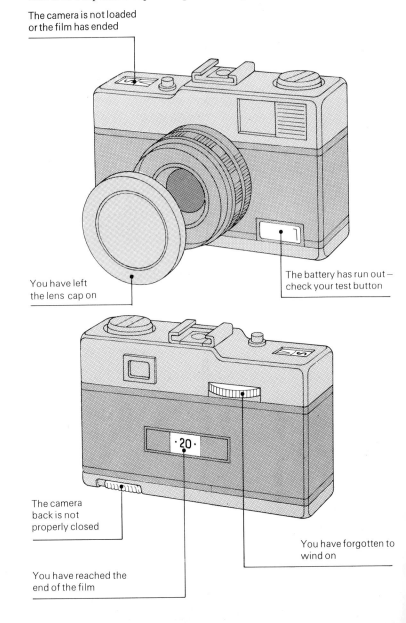

The camera is not loaded or the film has ended

You have left the lens cap on

The battery has run out — check your test button

The camera back is not properly closed

You have reached the end of the film

You have forgotten to wind on

35 mm cameras

There are several points to check as well as those shown in the illustration. Is the film winding on correctly? Are your camera's auto controls set correctly? Does the battery need replacing? You may not have activated the camera's exposure meter, which in turn cocks the shutter. Some models have a separate meter switch. On others you activate the meter with the shutter release or by pulling the wind-on lever clear of the camera body.

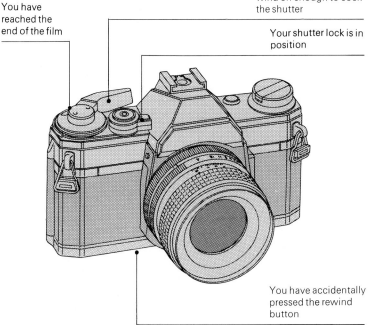

You have forgotten to wind on or have failed to wind on enough to cock the shutter

You have reached the end of the film

Your shutter lock is in position

You have accidentally pressed the rewind button

Instant picture cameras

On Kodak cameras, make sure that the batteries are not dead, or the film pack empty. With Polaroid models, check that the camera is loaded and that the flash bulbs are not finished. Some Polaroid models also have a shutter lock that stops the camera working in poor light.

Batteries

Most cameras use batteries to operate exposure meter, shutter, and in some cases built-in flash. Without reliable batteries the camera will be useless, so when buying and using batteries:

● Take a note from the packet of the type of batteries you use (the batteries themselves may be difficult to identify).

● Buy from a shop that tests the batteries for you.

● Use alkaline batteries.

● Install correctly, following the manufacturer's instructions.

● Clean contacts with a non-absorbent, soft, dry cloth.

● Remove batteries from the camera when you are not using it for long periods.

● Always replace the full set of batteries.

PICTURE FAULTS

Most well-known camera manufacturers produce reliable equipment capable of standing up to prolonged use by professional photographers. Budget-priced cameras will not take this kind of treatment, but if cared for and used correctly they will give years of trouble-free picture taking. Problems with your pictures usually arise from wrong handling. Use the following checklist to eliminate the most obvious of these:

● Check that you have set the correct ASA.
● With cameras that have the viewfinder separate from the lens, check that you have taken the lens cap off.
● Check that your camera and/or flash batteries are working.
● Check that the light level is adequate with simple cameras.
● Check that your subjects are within flash range.
● Make sure that you have set the correct synchronization speed when using flash.

(You should also check that your camera is working properly by reading the pages on Camera faults.) The commonest handling problems are illustrated below. Other reasons for disappointing or faulty prints or slides are incorrect processing of film and/or printing of negatives. If you think the processing laboratory is at fault, return your film or prints immediately and ask for an explanation. Common processing faults are also illustrated below.

Overexposure
This causes highlights, such as the sky, to become bleached out and colourless. Colours are generally murky and desaturated. Brings out detail in shadow areas. The problem can, to a degree, be compensated for during processing with print film, but not with slides.

Underexposure
This is the opposite to the fault above. Shadow areas are clogged and solid, but mid-tone and highlight areas show good detail. The colours and general mood of the picture are generally sombre. This also can be corrected to a degree if printed, but not on slide film.

Daylight film in tungsten light

An overall yellow cast results from using daylight-balanced film in tungsten lighting. The higher yellow content of tungsten light can be off-set by using an 80 filter over the camera lens. You get a similar effect when shooting in sunrises or sunsets.

Old film

This print was made from film that was either old or had been badly stored. There is always a date on your film packet that tells you when it should be processed by. Even new film will deteriorate if stored incorrectly.

Partly fogged

This film was probably loaded in bright sunlight. But this type of fogging can also be caused by light leaking into the camera. If the problem persists, consult your dealer at once.

Out of focus

This blurred image was caused by inaccurate focusing. With simple cameras, the focus symbols make mistakes quite likely. On SLRs this is not a problem as you can see if the image is sharp in the viewfinder.

Blur
This problem is caused by moving the camera when taking the picture. Either the shutter speed was too slow (1/30 second or slower), or the camera was not handled properly. On light weight cameras this is a particular problem, especially if you jab at the shutter release.

Sloping horizon
This very common framing fault is due simply to not keeping the camera parallel with the ground. The effect is particularly comical with water. Always take the time to see that horizons are straight.

Bad framing
When a processing laboratory prints your film, it uses a mask to hold your negatives in place. You must allow a little room for this when composing your picture. If all the information is on the negative, you can have it reprinted.

Double exposure
You will get overlapping images if your camera wind-on mechanism is faulty, or if the film has not been loaded properly. With most cameras, you cannot release the shutter until you have wound the film on

Obstruction
With 110, 126, and rangefinder cameras you do not view the scene through the lens but through the viewfinder. Make sure you keep fingers, camera strap, and camera case away from the lens or you will obstruct the view.

Vignetting
The wrong lens hood has obstructed the edges of the picture. Lens hoods are made to fit specific lenses and should not be interchanged.

Black spots
Spots like this can be caused by dirt inside the camera. Use a blower brush or can of compressed air to clean out any dust or grit. Take care not to damage the shutter with the nozzle of the can or scratch the black interior (this may cause flare).

Flare
This problem arises when direct sunlight (or artificial light) floods into the camera lens. Always use a lens hood in bright conditions, or change your position so as to eliminate the worst effects of direct light. You can sometimes use your free hand to shade the camera lens.

FLASH FAULTS
Burnt-out print
The fault on this print could have been caused in a number of ways. The subject may have been too close to the flash, the camera aperture may have been too large for a non-automatic flash, or too low an ASA number was set on an automatic flash gun.

Dark print
With this type of fault, the subject was too far from the flash, or the aperture was too small for the range of the flash. Alternatively, an automatic flash gun was used with too high an ASA speed.

Red eye
This problem is caused by the flash being too close to the lens of your camera, and is, in fact, a reflection from the blood vessels in the eye. With flash cubes, use an extender. With a flash gun, move it to one side and use a synch cord.

Glare
This is caused by flash light bouncing back from a window, mirror, or any reflective surface. If you can't avoid including glass or shiny surfaces in the background, try and shoot at a 45° angle.

Half-exposed print
This fault is produced by too fast a shutter speed. The shutter was closing before the flash fired. Check your hand-book for the correct speed. If your camera has both "X" and "M" settings, you should use "X" with electronic flash, and "M" for flash bulbs.

PROCESSOR FAULTS
Print cut-off
When you get one whole print and part of another on the same piece of paper, the processor's automatic guillotine has been wrongly set. You may also get two half prints together.

Black edge
This type of fault is usually due to the processor setting the negative mask incorrectly, so that part of the negative's edge has been printed as well.

Colour cast
The processor has probably set the wrong filtration when printing. First, check that your negative is satisfactory — a badly stored or old film could be the cause.

HOLIDAY CHECKLIST

Going on holiday represents an important opportunity to take pictures you will want to keep. Exotic sights and sounds tend to sharpen your perception of your surroundings, making every turn in the road a potential photograph. Although you should not burden yourself with unnecessary equipment, make sure you have plenty of film – there can be nothing so frustrating as running out of film during your trip.

Because the pictures you take on holiday are more than likely unrepeatable, you should prepare thoroughly. In a notebook, record details of your usual film, flash type, and both camera and flash batteries (if relevant), so that you know just what to ask for when they run out. Make sure your film is fresh, and if you have not changed batteries recently, buy spares. Depending on where you go, these things may be impossible to buy or a lot more expensive. For insurance purposes, make a complete list of all your equipment and accessories, noting down all model and serial numbers, and their value.

Use the checklist below to make sure nothing is forgotten.

Camera and film
Check and clean your camera and lens
Check your flash
Load a fresh film and have the old one developed

Documents to take with you
Receipts
Guarantees
Insurance forms

Basic equipment
Camera
Ever-ready case
Film
Ultraviolet or skylight filter
Lens hood and cap
Flash/flash bulbs
Notebook
Batteries for camera, flash, and motor drive/autowinder
Blower brush/lens cloth

Optional equipment
Spare lenses
Equipment case/shoulder bag
Mini tripod and cable release
Polarizing and special effects filters
Plastic bag and rubber bands for wet weather
Insulated bag for film and ice pack (for hot climates)

BUYING A CAMERA

There is an ever-increasing number of cameras on the market, and you should be able to find one that meets most of your requirements.

First of all
- Set yourself a budget and stick to it.
- Look in magazines and books which run lists of the cameras available and their prices.
- Decide which format suits your needs. For small prints a 110 will probably do. If you want good quality enlargements, or expect to take colour slides, a 35 mm camera will be best. A wider choice of film is also available for these cameras.
- Decide which type of camera you want. A compact can offer simple operation, built-in flash, and autofocus, but will provide only a limited range of accessories and, in most cases, no choice of lenses. A 35 mm SLR, with its wider range of accessories, and choice of interchangeable lenses, is far more versatile.
- Whichever camera you eventually choose, well-known manufacturers generally offer the best quality and after-sales service.

Choosing an SLR
- Do you want automatic or manual operation?
- Automatics include shutter priority, ideal for action shots (you select the shutter speed, the camera sets the aperture), and aperture priority (you select the aperture, the camera sets the shutter speed. Fully automatic models are also available.
- Multimode cameras offer both aperture and shutter priority operation, as well as manual and fully automatic options.
- A manual camera with a built-in light meter gives you total exposure control.
- Beware of paying too much for features you will be unlikely to use.

Assessing additional needs
- Try to decide what sort of pictures you want to take.
- Are there accessories to help? Many makes of camera have only a limited range. You may want a macro lens for close-up work, or a motor drive for action photography.
- Try to assess your future needs, and decide whether the cameras you have selected can cope with them.
- Using these points, try to limit your choice to about three cameras.

Buying your camera
- Go to a camera shop, and ask to see the cameras on your list.
- They may look very similar, but the controls and other features will differ. Examine these carefully.
- Handle each camera. Do they fit comfortably in the hand? Are the controls accessible and easy to use?
- At this point one camera should seem right for you.
- When you buy the camera, make sure you have the batteries.
- If the camera does not have a protective case, buy one.

EXPOSURE DATA

The necessary exposure settings for particular weather conditions vary according to the sensitivity of your film (its "speed"). The table below gives the best settings for a range of commonly used films. If your film is not listed, compare its ASA speed with those below. A film of similar speed will require similar exposure settings. The settings given are averages for each situation. If you are not sure which to use, you can always try bracketing (setting exposure one stop either side of the recommended exposure as well as using the "correct" setting).

Some new films allow you to use them at a range of ASA speeds. These are black and white films, known as "chromogenic" films. They can be processed by your usual laboratory. The ASA speeds for these two films indicate the manufacturers' suggested ranges, although the films will produce their best results at the lower end of the range. The settings are those suggested at the maximum ASA ratings for each film. These films are the only ones which allow you to use this wide range of settings on one film.

	Film speed (ASA)	Bright sun/hazy sun with distinct shadows	Weak, hazy sun, soft shadows	Cloudy, bright, no shadows	Open shade/heavily overcast
Slow films (25–64 ASA)					
Kodachrome 25	25	f8 at 1/125 sec	f5.6 at 1/125 sec	f4 at 1/125 sec	f2.8 at 1/125 sec
Kodak Panatomic-X	32				
Agfachrome CT18	50				
Agfacolor CNS	80				
Agfacolor CT18	50	f11 at 1/125 sec	f8 at 1/125 sec	f5.6 at 1/125 sec	f4 at 1/125 sec
Ilford Pan F	50				
Kodachrome 64	64				
Kodak Ektachrome 64	64				
Medium films (100–200 ASA)					
Agfachrome CT21	100				
Agfacolor CN100	100				
Boots Colourprint 2	100				
Fujichrome 100RD	100				
Ilford FP4	125	f11 at 1/250 sec	f8 at 1/250 sec	f5.6 at 1/250 sec	f4 at 1/250 sec
Kodacolor II	100				
Kodak Plus-X Pan	125				
Kodak Verichrome Pan	125				
3M Colorslide 100	100				
Agfachrome 200	200	f16 at 1/250 sec	f11 at 1/250 sec	f8 at 1/250 sec	f5.6 at 1/250 sec
Kodak Ektachrome 200	200				
Fast films (400 ASA)					
Agfacolor CNS400	400				
Boots Colourprint 400	400				
Fujichrome 400	400				
Fujicolor 400	400				
Ilford HP5	400	f16 at 1/500 sec	f11 at 1/500 sec	f8 at 1/500 sec	f5.6 at 1/500 sec
Kodacolor 400	400				
Kodak Ektachrome 400	400				
Kodak Tri-X Pan	400				
3M Colorprint 400	400				
3M Colorslide 400	400				
Chromogenic films					
Agfa Vario XL	125–1600	—	f22 at 1/500 sec	f16 at 1/500 sec	f11 at 1/500 sec
Ilford XP1	200–800	f22 at 1/500 sec	f16 at 1/500 sec	f11 at 1/500 sec	f8 at 1/500 sec

FILTER DATA

Most colour filters affect the intensity of light reaching the film, but if your camera has TTL (through-the-lens) metering it will take account of the reduction in light. Even so, you need to compensate to varying degrees with different types of colour filter. Red filters, graduated filters, and mask filters, shaped to represent keyholes, binocular vision, or other framing effects, each require considerable exposure compensation. TTL meters are slightly less sensitive to red filters than to other colours and may cause underexposure when one is used. Graduated filters can also mislead an in-camera meter, so that you obtain a slight overexposure of the unfiltered areas and a slight underexposure of the areas filtered by the coloured portion. With this type of filter it is best to "bracket", exposing according to the meter's reading and then shooting one stop either side of its recommended exposure. With mask filters you should measure exposure before fitting and then bracket as well. Clear filters do not normally reduce the incoming light. The table shows the exposure compensation, in f stops, required with a selection of popular filters. The figures given are approximate. Where available, the filter manufacturer's recommended exposure compensation should be used.

Filter	Effect	Exposure compensation (f stops)
Ultraviolet Skylight	Reduction of effect of haze and of blue cast caused by snow or clear blue sky. Useful as lens protector.	—
Polarizing	Reduction of glare from non-metallic reflective surfaces, such as glass and water. Darkening of blue sky and other colours with colour film.	$+1\frac{1}{2}$
80	Prevention of yellow cast when used with daylight film in tungsten light.	$+1$
85	Prevention of blue cast when used with tungsten film in daylight.	$+\frac{1}{2}$
81	Warming when used with Ektachrome film in hazy conditions or for portraits or "glamour" effect.	$+\frac{1}{2}$
Yellow	Darkening of blue sky, to increase contrast with clouds, with black and white film.	$+\frac{1}{2}-1$
Orange	Intensifies effect of yellow filter with black and white film.	$+1-1\frac{1}{2}$
Red	Intensifies effect of orange filter with black and white film.	$+2\frac{1}{2}-3$
Centre spot	Diffuse, coloured surround, with clear centre spot for main subject.	—
Diffraction	Highlights split into the colours of the spectrum.	—
Diffusion	Softening of colour and focus.	—
Starburst	Highlights split into star shapes with variable number of radiations.	—
Multi-image	Repetition and overlapping of image.	—
Split field	Simultaneous focus on different depths within a scene.	—
Close-up	Magnification of image size	—

SELLING YOUR PICTURES

From time to time you may take pictures which are of interest to a newspaper, or other publication.

Amateurs who work for a company with a staff newspaper or magazine have an advantage in starting to sell their work. These publications are always interested in pictures relating to the firm's activities, and it is usually very easy for you to make contact with the people who produce them. You will probably find that they pay a set fee for the photographs they reproduce. For a newspaper they will want to use black and white prints. Colour magazines work from transparencies.

Your local newspaper will often be pleased to get pictures of events they were unable to cover. Again, they will want to use black and white prints. If you think you have an interesting shot, you should first phone the editor. Don't expect fees to be high, and local papers may not buy at all if your picture is simply promoting a local interest group.

If you think you have a picture that is important, leave the film in your camera, and telephone one of the national newspapers. Ask for the picture desk, and tell them what you think you have, and which film, camera, and lens you used. Then ask them to phone you back.

If they want to use your picture, ask how much they are willing to pay. If you sell them the picture outright, you will probably get a fair deal, but you will not be able to make more money by selling the picture elsewhere. Alternatively, you could sell them the UK rights, and keep the rights for the rest of the world for yourself. It is usually easier to sell the UK rights, with an option for the rest of the world. A national paper has the contacts to sell your pictures for you elsewhere.

It is impossible to predict how much a picture will be worth. An exclusive shot of an event of international importance could fetch thousands of pounds. But most other pictures would be worth much less. Some papers will try to pay very little. If you are unhappy with an offer, refuse it, and contact another newspaper – quickly.

When you have agreed on terms, the newspaper will tell you how to get the undeveloped film to them. If you deliver it, ask for a receipt giving details of what is on the film and the terms you have agreed. Otherwise, ask someone else to confirm it with them by phone.

INDEX

Figures in **bold** type indicate main entries.

ACKNOWLEDGMENTS

I would like to thank Graham Watts and Peter Cook at Yorkshire Television, and all the contributors to the programme, for their help and example; Sally Mason at Trident for holding my hand; Joss, Stuart, and Richard at Dorling Kindersley for their understanding and energy; and everyone in the photographic business – in particular Colin Rogers of Photomasters, Liz Royal and Phil Lawrence of Kodak, Andy Parkhouse of Polaroid, and Harry Collins of Nikon – for their friendly advice and assistance.

Joe Partridge

Dorling Kindersley Limited would like to give special thanks to:
Rosamund Gendle, Jonathan Hilton, Laurie Parker, and Phil Wilkinson.

Technical assistance: Agfa-Gevaert Ltd, Boots Co Ltd, DG Leisure Centres, Fujimex (UK) Ltd, Ilford Ltd, Kodak Ltd, Konishiroku UK, Polaroid (UK) Ltd, 3M UK Ltd

Photographs:
Heather Angel
Derry Brabbs
John Bulmer
Ed Buziak
Peter Cook
Richard Dawes
Andrew de Lory
Joanna Godfrey Wood
Alan Harbour
George Hughes
Stuart Jackman
Simon Jennings
Peter Kindersley
Sarah King
Patrick Lichfield
Joe Partridge
David Pearson
Erik Pelham
Chris Smith
Homer Sykes
Yorkshire Television

Patrick Lichfield's portrait of Sir John Mills (p. 89) was taken for the cover of Sir John's book *"Up in the Clouds, Gentlemen Please"* and is used by kind courtesy of the publisher, Weidenfeld and Nicolson.

Further reading: The Book of Photography, The Photographer's Handbook, The Step by Step Guide to Photography, The Book of Colour Photography, The SLR Handbook, The Pocket Camera Handbook, The Instant Picture Camera Handbook, (all published by Ebury Press).

Typesetting: Metro Reprographics Limited, London
Reproduction: Royal Smeets Offset B.V., Weert